The Living Word

AUDREY J. WILLIAMSON

THE LIVING WORD

A Study of the Public Reading of the Bible

Beacon Hill Press of Kansas City
Kansas City, Missouri

Copyright 1987
by Beacon Hill Press of Kansas City

Paperback Edition published in 2018
ISBN: 978-0-08341-3760-8

The Foundry Publishing
P.O. Box 419527
Kansas City, MO 64141
TheFoundryPublishing.com

All rights reserved.

Permission to quote from the following copyrighted versions is acknowledged with appreciation:

The Bible: An American Translation (Goodspeed), J. M. Powis Smith, Edgar J. Goodspeed. Copyright 1923, 1927, 1948 by the University of Chicago Press.

The Bible: A New Translation (Moffatt), copyright 1954 by James A. R. Moffatt. By permission of Harper and Row, Publishers, Inc.

New King James Version (NKJV), copyright © 1979, 1980, 1982, Thomas Nelson, Inc., Publishers.

New Testament in Modern English (Phillips), Revised Edition © J. B. Phillips, 1958, 1960, 1972. By permission of the Macmillan Publishing Co.

Revised Standard Version of the Bible (RSV), copyrighted 1946, 1952, © 1971, 1973.

The Weymouth New Testament in Modern Speech (Weymouth), copyright 1929 by Harper and Brothers, New York.

Also quoted: *The Emphasized Bible,* by J. B. Rotherham, 1902, 1916.

Contents

Foreword	7
Preface	9
THE SIGNIFICANCE OF READING THE BIBLE ALOUD	13
PREPARATION FOR READING THE BIBLE ALOUD	19

Determine the literary style • Get the background • Understand the language • Arrive at the meaning • Personal readiness of the reader • Arrange the Scripture passages • Final preparation

THE VOICES OF THE BIBLE	33
The Voice of the Interpreter	35

Faults in tone production • Expressive actions of the voice

The Voices of the Storytellers	49

The historians • The users of parables • The dramatists

The Voices of the Teachers	69

The users of proverbs • The letter writers • The Master Teacher

The Voices of the Poets	85
The Voices of the Prophets	93
The Voices of Sublime Truth	103

The great affirmations • The emotions of Jesus • The great prayers • The great benedictions • The seven last words of Jesus

Appendix	141

Foreword

To congregations and audiences in the Church of the Nazarene around the world, probably the most keenly remembered oral interpreter of God's written Word is the author of this book—Audrey J. Williamson.

Few will forget the impression of a small woman moving to the speaker's stand, squaring her shoulders, turning her head just a bit, and declaring, "Who hath believed our report? and to whom is the arm of the Lord revealed?" (Isa. 53:1) with the unmistakable authority of a prophet.

For years students and friends urged Audrey Williamson to expand the parameters of her classroom by putting her thoughts on oral interpretation of the Bible on paper. For as many years she was too busy professionally, as well as being the wife of a pastor, an educator, and a general superintendent—all the same man, G. B. Williamson. (Incidentally, Dr. Williamson was a one-time student of Audrey's, and always her greatest supporter.)

When initially approached, the publisher questioned how a subject of this sort could fill the length requirements of a book. That query was quickly dismissed when the author submitted her working outline. A hasty glance at the contents page will bear this out.

The work's audience will include all who must read aloud selections not only from the Bible but also from other serious prose and poetry works.

Mrs. Williamson's personal declamation style may not fit every interpreter, but the principles of interpretation she shares will provide students, ministers, and lay readers alike with a clear-cut rationale for, and practical instructions in, public reading. The illustrations from all parts of the Bible and the arrangements of scripture found in the Appendix are a worship leader's treasure.

—The Publisher

Preface

My Background for Writing This Book

My mother found the Lord as Savior when I was four years old. At once the Word of God became for her exceedingly precious. It was her Guide, her Counselor, her inspiration, her Director. She read it for pleasure; she studied it for instruction; she memorized it for meditation. It was her constant Companion. When she was doing dishes, it was propped up over the kitchen sink. When she was ironing, it was open on the head of the ironing board. Many times I have seen her scrub the kitchen floor on her hands and knees (the only way to really get it clean), pushing the Bible ahead of her as long as there was a dry spot. She loved the Word of God!

And she took seriously the command in Deut. 6:6-7:

> These words, which I command thee this day, shall be in thine heart: and thou shalt teach them diligently unto thy children, and shalt talk of them when thou sittest in thine house, and when thou walkest by the way, and when thou liest down, and when thou risest up.

Daily she had for me and my sister, who was four years older, what she called our "child's altar." Our textbook was the Word. We read it, we studied it, we memorized it. We became familiar with its form and its content. We had drills to see who could find a given passage first. She followed Paul's guidelines: "Give attendance to reading, to exhortation, to doctrine" (1 Tim. 4:13). She took us through *Binney's Theological Compend with References* before I was into my teens.

I left home for college when I had just turned 17. In my freshman year, I registered for a course in Bible reading taught by Miss T. Bell Chambers. She was a student of Dr. S. S. Curry, who founded the School of Expression in Boston. Miss Chambers used his text, *Vocal and Literary Interpretation of the Bible.* And now I was introduced to a new concept—the Bible as literature, the Bible capable of oral interpretation. For four years I studied under these teachers, and then I began teaching others myself.

By now, the Word of God had become a very vital part of my life. I was memorizing and interpreting longer portions. My mother had had us commit to memory scores of verses. Now I began to recite such passages as Psalms 27; 32; 91; 103; Isaiah 12; 35; 53; 55; 1 Corinthians 13; Revelation 22; and many more.

It was while my husband, Gideon Williamson, was president of Eastern Nazarene College in Quincy, Mass., that he said to me one day, "I am to conduct a school promotion service at our district assembly tomorrow. I want you to read the scripture." "Which one?" I asked. "Isaiah 40," he replied. I reviewed it carefully in the next 24 hours and recited it, as requested, the following day.

This experience seemed to serve as a launching pad for the public reading of the Word of God for me. Al Ramquist and P. H. Lunn were in that assembly, representing the Nazarene Publishing House. They both encouraged me to continue this special ministry. Dr. James B. Chapman was the presiding general superintendent. He, too, offered his commendation.

Following my husband's retirement in 1968 from the general superintendency with the Church of the Nazarene, we offered our services to the Nazarene Bible College, Colorado Springs, as instructors, he in the field of Bible and I in speech communication. I had taught the oral reading of the Scriptures for many years at both John Fletcher College in Iowa and Eastern Nazarene College in Massachusetts. Again at Nazarene Bible College I organized the class for second-year students in reading the Bible. The need of an appropriate textbook for this class impelled me to attempt to produce one. Circumstances brought about delays.

It was Bob Benson who finally nudged me to offer my project for publication. His persistent enthusiasm for the oral interpretation of God's Word encouraged me. Ronald Attig, who teaches the subject at Nazarene Bible College, had never really given up on my getting the work finished, though I am sure he had often lost heart. His wife, Ann, had helped type the rough draft, and Ron himself had plowed through the manuscript numbers of times with me. My final confirmation was in securing Bonnie Wiseman to put it in proper form. To all of these patient people I give thanks.

This volume has in mind particularly men and women who will be reading the Bible publicly and who are seeking to improve their rendition. Hopefully it can be used as a text in Bible colleges and seminaries. But it should also be useful to any layman seeking to improve his reading skills. It is a "how to" book. It seeks by its very simplicity to open the Word and challenge the reader to its effective oral presentation.

There is an absolute joy in the meaningful interpretation of God's Word orally so that speaker and hearers are caught up in the contemplation of its majestic truths. Because it was first presented to us as the spoken word, this text emphasizes the Voices—the Voice of the Interpreter, the Voices of the Storytellers, the Teachers, the Poets, the Prophets, and the Voices of Sublime Truth.

It is my earnest desire and prayer that this book shall open up the Bible to many who have until now only engaged in the silent or the perfunctory reading of the Word of God.

THE SIGNIFICANCE OF READING THE BIBLE ALOUD

The Significance of Reading the Bible Aloud

The Bible was spoken before it was written. The confessed authorship of the Scriptures, as they themselves declare, is that "holy men of God spake as they were moved by the Holy [Spirit]" (2 Pet. 1:21). The Bible is the Word of God. He is its divine Author.

IT WAS WRITTEN TO BE READ ALOUD

But it was first given orally. The historical books were narrated before they were transcribed, as were the accounts recorded in the Gospels. The prophets thundered forth their messages orally before they were reduced to writing. The Psalms were sung; the Proverbs were repeated from generation to generation. The Epistles were written to be read in the churches (see Col. 4:16).

It is fitting, then, that attention be given to reading aloud the Word of the Lord.

This text will practically fail in its purpose for being written unless the reader takes the suggestions given and tries them aloud for himself. One cannot perfect his vocal interpretation of the Bible by silently reading it in his study any more than a singer can perfect his art by sitting in the library and reading a book about Caruso. No! You will need to practice aloud! Just as a violinist tunes his instrument, then spends many arduous hours rehearsing before he attempts a concert ap-

YOU'LL HAVE TO TRY IT

pearance, so we as readers of the Word must bring voice and body, mind and spirit into the captivity of this marvelous message of eternal truth. As we give ourselves to this task, the Bible will come alive, and we will reach a degree of fulfillment that is breathtaking. But it must be done aloud. I challenge you to try it.

This practice is not new. Before printing presses made copies of the Bible easily accessible, the Bible was read aloud when worshipers gathered together in order that its message might be shared by all who were interested in hearing it. The reading of the Scriptures is an accepted part of public worship services today. In many homes the Bible is read aloud each day as part of family worship. Increased interest in classes that give attention to a study of the art of public Bible reading is evidenced in college and seminary curricula. A resurgence of the effective interpretation of the Word of God through the human voice could have a powerful effect upon the times in which we live. Hopefully, such public reading of the Bible will not only captivate the hearers at the moment but will impel them to "seek . . . out of the book of the Lord, and read" for themselves in private as well (Isa. 34:16). A return to the reading of the Word of God is a crying need in our day.

Woodrow Wilson, president of Princeton University and 28th president of the United States, stated: "I am sorry for the men who do not read the Bible every day; I wonder why they deprive themselves of the strength and of the pleasure. It is one of the most singular books in the world, for every time you open it, some old text that you have read a score of times suddenly beams with a new meaning. There is no other book that I know of, of which this is true; there is no other book that yields its meaning so personally, that seems to fit itself so intimately to the very spirit that is seeking its guidance."

William Lyon Phelps in 1957 declared: "Everyone who has a thorough knowledge of the Bible may truly be called educated; and no other learning or culture, no matter how extensive or elegant, can, among Europeans and Americans, form a proper substitute. Western civilization is founded upon the Bible; our ideas, our wisdom, our philosophy, our art, our ideals come more from the Bible than from all other books put together."

PREPARATION FOR READING THE BIBLE ALOUD

Preparation for Reading the Bible Aloud

The Bible is a library of 66 books. To be fully appreciated, it must be recognized as a literary masterpiece. True, its message is primarily moral and religious. It points the way of righteous living and sets forth the folly and danger of unrighteousness. But it expresses these timeless truths in literary forms. Its purposes are set forth by prophets and poets, by lawgivers and statisticians, by historians and storytellers. In studying the Bible as literature, we are exploring the product of 47 different minds and their varied ways of describing man's relationship to God. Their motives in speaking were different, and the literary form in which they expressed themselves was consequently different. Only a literary study of the Bible will reveal this, and only the human voice can adequately differentiate these impelling motives.

THE BIBLE IS LITERATURE

The voice of the interpreter can give meaning and significance to the passage read. It can arouse feeling and deepen the impact of sublime truth. A man of profound intellectual capacity said when he heard the 40th chapter of Isaiah read aloud with true appreciation of its literary and spiritual values, "It is as though I had been handed a commentary."

Determine the Literary Style

In determining the type of literature in which a passage is written, we are assisted by examination of its form. Though in the older versions of the Bible its poetry is not printed in verse form, an oral reading of poetic passages immediately gives one a sense of their rhythm.

> Lift up your heads, O ye gates;
> Even lift them up, ye everlasting doors;
> And the King of glory shall come in *(Ps. 24:9)*.

Sense the difference in form with the oral reading of this passage.

> Cry aloud, spare not, lift up thy voice like a trumpet, and shew my people their transgression, and the house of Jacob their sins *(Isa. 58:1)*.

This latter form indicates the prophet, the preacher, the crusader for righteousness with his short, dynamic phrases, his telling figures, his persuasive appeal.

Sense yet another literary form in the following:

> A certain man had two sons: and the younger of them said to his father, Father, give me the portion of goods that falleth to me. And he divided unto them his living *(Luke 15:11-12)*.

The simple, direct language, the flow of events, the introduction of personalities reveal still another literary form—that of the story or narrative.

But perhaps a surer and more decisive way of determining the literary type is to arrive at the *purpose* of the writer in selecting that particular medium for his message. Is his purpose to extol or to persuade, to warn or to interest, to instruct or to suggest a hidden truth, to pour out a flood of emotion or to lift to the sublime? Various literary forms lend themselves to the varying purposes of the speakers or writers. An intensive study of the passage involved, with a genuine effort to correctly interpret its purpose, will save public Bible reading from becoming a dull, monotonous mumbling of incomparable truth and make it even more than a literary masterpiece. It will become "the

PURPOSE DETERMINES STYLE

living Word." "The letter killeth, but the spirit giveth life" (2 Cor. 3:6).

Likewise, the *material* of the different literary forms will vary. If people predominate, the form is drama; if events, the form is historical or narrative; if assertions of truth are most evident, we are in the literature of the teachers or the prophets.

MATERIAL DETERMINES STYLE

Get the Background

Knowledge of the setting for a Bible passage before it can adequately be interpreted is essential. What were the circumstances that produced it? Where and when was it first declared? Bible histories and commentaries will assist the reader at this point. Is the speaker in a hostile or a friendly atmosphere? Are circumstances favorable or unpleasant? What has gone before?

In many cases, it is helpful even to have a thorough knowledge of the topography of the country. Distances become important. We need also to be familiar with the customs and culture of the people involved. Times have changed since the Bible was written, and we only mouth words if we do not know the significance and the meaning of many biblical allusions.

Psalm 23 and John 10 have long been favorite passages for millions of people. Those who have made the effort to inform themselves of the unique and intimate relationship existing between the oriental shepherd and his sheep have a deeper appreciation of these lovely scriptures. The figure of the Bible-land shepherd with his horn of oil, his rod to control, and his staff to rescue must be vivid in the mind of the reader as he says, "I am the good shepherd" (John 10:11, 14). The true keeper of sheep knows each by name, feeds them, defends them, rests them, calls to them with a distinctive cry that no hireling can imitate. Safely he guides them through dark canyons and over precipitous mountain passes. Out into the night he goes to seek and to find a lost sheep. Agitation, insecurity, fear, and distrust vanish in the close presence of the shepherd.

When a reader has thoroughly saturated his mind and soul with the atmosphere and spirit of a passage, how can the voice convey this hidden meaning without oral exegesis? I do not know! I cannot explain it! But I know it is true. I have heard it happen over and over again with my students and in my own personal experience.

Here is another example of the importance of knowing background. Psalm 51 can be correctly interpreted only when the reader realizes that those heartbroken petitions poured forth from the lips of David, the king, after Nathan, the prophet, had exposed his sin of adultery with Bathsheba and of murder in the slaying of her husband, Uriah, as recorded in 2 Samuel 11 and 12. Hear David's bitter comment:

PLEASE! WON'T YOU GIVE IT A TRY?

> Have mercy upon me, O God, according to thy lovingkindness: according unto the multitude of thy tender mercies blot out my transgressions.
>
> Wash me throughly from mine iniquity, and cleanse me from my sin.
>
> For I acknowledge my transgressions: and my sin is ever before me. . . . .
>
> Create in me a clean heart, O God; and renew a right spirit within me. . . .
>
> Restore unto me the joy of thy salvation; and uphold me with thy free spirit. . . .
>
> The sacrifices of God are a broken spirit: a broken and a contrite heart, O God, thou wilt not despise *(Ps. 51:1-3, 10, 12, 17).*

A very able and serious-minded student of mine brought this selection of Scripture to me at a private lesson some years ago. She was preparing to read it in public. Her oral interpretation was cold and empty, devoid of a real awareness of the depth of David's guilt and remorse.

I told her, "Hazel, you will never read this passage well until you feel like an adulterer and a murderer."

She was shocked. "I can't do it," she gasped.

"All right," I replied, "change your selection."

But she was challenged. The following week when she returned for her lesson, she was still with Psalm 51, but her reading of the passage moved me to tears. It was not sensational and artificial. It represented a genuine "othering" of herself as she realized the depths of David's plea for restoration. Later when she read the passage in public, she moved her audience as she had moved me. There is no substitute for genuine participation as we read the Word of God.

Understand the Language

The King James Version of the Bible was translated in the 16th century. It is not surprising that the meanings of words have changed and that after four centuries usage is not the same. Forms now archaic sometimes appear. To adjust the language of Scripture until it is understandable does not do violence if the strict meaning of the passage is preserved. For instance, in common usage in the Bible is the word "spake," the past tense of the verb "to speak." If this bothers the tongue of the reader, let him use the word "spoke" instead. However, it is true that oral practice of the more formal diction of the King James Version will give the reader ease in reading it until the form is not a hindrance.

It is an invaluable exercise, moreover, to acquaint oneself with the various versions of translations of the Scripture. These shed light upon the interpretation of the passage for the reader and, consequently, his hearers.

COMPARISON OF VARIOUS VERSIONS Among standard translations of the Scripture are the recognized works of James Moffatt, Richard Weymouth, Edgar Goodspeed, J. B. Rotherham, as well as the *Revised Standard Version*, the *New American Standard Bible*, the *New English Bible*, the *New Berkeley Version*, and the *New International Version*. The *New Testament in Modern English*, by J. B. Phillips, is illuminating, as well as the paraphrase known as *The Living Bible*.

A brief illustration of how these versions can clarify meaning follows:

In 1 Cor. 13:4-5, the King James Version, in describing "charity," says it "vaunteth not itself, is not puffed up." Weymouth translates this passage, "Love does not brag"; Moffatt reads, "Love makes no parade"; Goodspeed says, "It does not put on airs." The *Revised Standard Version* has "It is not arrogant"; Phillips interprets the passage, "Nor does it cherish inflated ideas of its own importance."

Thus light is shed on the passage for the one preparing to read it regardless of what version he chooses to use for his oral presentation. The Scripture portions used in this text are all taken from the King James Version. This happens to be the version most familiar to the author. But the chief reason for the decision is that every reader may now feel free to choose the particular version most acceptable to him for the reading of any particular passage.

Arrive at the Meaning

The Bible is unique in that behind its various literary forms there lie deep spiritual truths applicable to the individual listener. The Word of God has a message. It speaks to the need of the human heart. It is history, it is allegory, it is poetry, it is drama; but more than literature, it is eternal truth. It is God's message to man. It has universal application. The oral interpreter is responsible for determining this hidden meaning and illuminating it by the expressive actions of his voice and body.

Some schools of thought will differ at this point. They insist that the Scriptures themselves warn against "private interpretation" (2 Pet. 1:20); that they should be presented without any persuasion on the part of the reader; that cold, impersonal, unfeeling form leaves hearers free to supply their own interpretation.

But I submit to you that hearers won't supply their own interpretations. They will only be bored and distracted by the monotonous drone of the speaker's voice. That which is living and vital and quickening will be stifled by the manner of its presentation. And do you adopt this attitude toward the interpretation of any other literature? If we are seeking to interpret Shakespeare or Wordsworth or Tennyson or Daniel Webster, do we not make an exhaustive effort to arrive at the meaning and purpose of his discourse and to faithfully portray it to the listening audience? The Word of God is sacred. But it is also the most vital, living, dynamic book ever written. It can be infused with energy and power by those who read it aloud.

READING MAKES IT COME ALIVE

Personal Readiness of the Reader

And the ultimate in preparation for the oral interpretation of the Bible is the illumination that comes to the individual from the Spirit of God himself. "When he, the Spirit of truth, is come, he will guide you into all truth" (John 16:13). The living presence of the Spirit of God in the soul and personality of the reader supplies a dimension to the reading of the Word that can be imparted in no other way.

THERE MUST BE A PLUS

A man well trained in the art of public speaking quoted Psalm 23 on a given occasion. His diction was perfect. The changes of volume and rate and pitch were flawless, yet his reading left his hearers cold and unmoved. Later, a devout and simple man, untrained in the techniques of communication, recited the same psalm:

> The Lord is my shepherd; I shall not want.
>
> He maketh me to lie down in green pastures: he leadeth me beside the still waters.
>
> He restoreth my soul . . .
>
> Surely goodness and mercy shall follow me all the days of my life: and I will dwell in the house of the Lord for ever.

Every hearer was deeply moved. Tears shone in the eyes of many. The familiar words had come alive.

"Explain the difference," one asked.

"Ah," came the answer. "The first reader knew the psalm. The second knew the Shepherd."

Arrange the Scripture Passages

The Bible is the inspired Word of God. But the arbitrary division into chapters and verses is not inspired. In fact, it can prove to be a hindrance to effective oral presentation if it is adhered to blindly. It is a convenience for locating a passage. That is its chief function.

CHAPTER AND VERSE DIVISION IS NOT INSPIRED

For example, 1 Corinthians 13 has been designated as the "love chapter," and indeed it is the most exalted description of love ever composed. In verses 1 to 3, Paul tells us what love *is not*. It is not eloquence or knowledge or mountain-moving faith or philanthropy or voluntary martyrdom.

In verses 4 to 7, Paul tells us what love *is*. It is patient, kind, humble, well behaved, selfless, magnanimous, and unfailing. And in verses 8 to 13, Paul tells us what love *shall be* when human limitations are dropped and we revel in the ineffable wonder of the more abundant life that is to come.

But the climax of the whole 13th chapter is found in the first three words of the 14th chapter—direct, incisive, commanding: *"Follow after [love]."*

This is the point and purpose of the marvelous revelations of chapter 13 that are given us, not merely to shame us for our loveless lives, but to challenge us to make love the consuming drive and purpose of our being. The oral interpreter will do well to conclude with "Follow after love" in his reading of 1 Corinthians 13.

DON'T BE AFRAID TO REARRANGE SCRIPTURE PASSAGES

Sometimes meaning is enhanced by omitting phrases that are repetitious or parenthetical. Likewise, certain passages are made more understandable and more chronologically accurate if they are rearranged. First John 1 may be rearranged to provide clarity and climax.

1 That which was from the beginning, of the Word of life
3 which we have seen and heard, declare we unto you, that ye also may have fellowship with us: and truly our fellowship is with the Father, and with his Son Jesus Christ.

5 This then is the message which we have heard of him, and declare unto you, that God is light, and in him is no darkness at all.

6 If we say that we have fellowship with him, and walk in darkness, we lie, and do not the truth:

10 If we say that we have not sinned, we make him a liar, and his word is not in us. 9 But if we confess our sins, he is faithful and just to forgive us our sins, and to cleanse us from all unrighteousness.

8 If we say that we have no sin, we deceive ourselves, and the truth is not in us. 7 But if we walk in the light, as he is in the light, we have fellowship one with another, and the blood of Jesus Christ his Son cleanseth us from all sin.

The omissions do not detract from the significance of the passage but rather improve its progression. And the rearrangement of verses makes the meaning more clear and climactic.

Perhaps there has been a limited number of individuals who have used the unprincipled practice of rearranging scriptures to prove their personal, prejudiced points of view. This is dishonest and culpable. But it *is* justifiable to lift up passages from various portions of the Bible that relate to a given theme and position them progressively in chronological order or as regards subject matter to emphasize a given title or to cement the relationship of truths.

This can be illustrated by combining passages from Numbers 14 and Joshua 14 that relate one exciting event in the life of Caleb, God's servant, in the days of ancient Israel. They may be arranged to make a stirring reading under the title "Give Me This Mountain" (see Appendix).

Final Preparation

Familiarity with the Bible in its entirety is, in the last analysis, the final step in preparation to intelligently and adequately read the Word aloud. This is a lifetime, never-to-be-completed assignment. One who wishes to portray the Bible message orally to others must study its history, acquaint himself with its personalities, be aware of its deeper meaning, revel in its imagery, open his mind to its personal applications, digest its truths, and acquire a deep love for it as the Book of books. To truly read the Word, one must live in the Word until he can say with Job, "I have esteemed the words of his mouth more than my necessary food" (Job 23:12); and with David, "How love I thy law!" (Ps. 119:97) and "Thy word is a lamp unto my feet, and a light unto my path" (v. 105).

The reader of a particular passage will be giving himself the most thorough and far-reaching preparation as he becomes a student of the whole Word of God. His love for it, his appreciation of it, his understanding of its timeless truth will transcend his love and appreciation for and understanding of any other book. The Bible becomes for him the living Word.

The effective reader of the Word of God must have an impelling desire to share its message with others. It is God's message to man, but it is channeled through the reader's personality, his voice, his eyes, his facial expression, his bodily response. Men have shied away from this concept of scriptural communication. They have allowed the sacredness of God's Word to intimidate them and cause them to read it with aloofness and detachment. We do not need to degenerate the Bible in order to communicate its truths. Instead of dragging its sublime message down to our human level, can we not elevate our minds and spirits to attain at least in a measure its lofty heights?

DO YOU REALLY WANT TO COMMUNICATE?

This concept will give the reader a desire for complete rapport with his audience, and he will employ the best techniques of communication. Even though he is reading, he should be familiar enough with the script to use eye directness. His body should respond to the varying moods of the passage he is interpreting. There will be a minimum of gesture, which is the lowest form of physical response anyway. But there will be a maximum response of the intrinsic musculature of the body. There will be a minimum of direct impersonation, but there will be a maximum of sympathetic participation.

In reading the passages found in John 19, verses 15 and 16, note the almost unobservable responses of bodily texture that accompany the words "Away with him, crucify him" and these words, "They took Jesus, and led him away." The total response of the reader to this scene will produce in his reading of the passage a genuineness, an authenticity that is convincing.

GET ALONE AND TRY IT

Such response can be developed by the reader through an earnest effort to thoroughly participate in every passage read. Inhibitions and prejudices must be dropped. I have known persons so overcome by the weight of a passage as to be rendered speechless with emotion. And yet when they gained control again, the voice came out cold and unfeeling. We need to harness our emotions and make them expressive of deepest meaning. We need to treasure our tears. Certainly a reader must respond within the framework of his own personality. It is not imitation we plead for nor yet exaggeration. Good taste will guide you.

AVOID THE EXTREMES— OVERDONE AND UNDERDONE

But in attempting to interpret God's message to man through His Holy Word, we need to be mastered by it until it possesses us, and we become God's mouthpiece to hungry, needy, disillusioned, groping humanity.

THE VOICES OF THE BIBLE

The Voice of the Interpreter

Before we can properly discuss the voices of the Bible speakers whom we are seeking to represent, we need to take a look at our own voices as would-be interpreters or readers.

The human voice is one of life's greatest miracles. Its capability of producing pleasing and intelligible speech, of projecting itself to be heard by a sizable audience even without amplification, of differentiation in meaning by changes of pitch and of rate, and of rousing emotion by its variations in quality challenge one to a lifetime of study.

THE HUMAN VOICE—A MARVELOUS MECHANISM

Since we cannot remember when we learned to talk, we have become accustomed to our own voices and to our particular diction. We are not, therefore, good judges of our own vocal excellences, and it will be beneficial if we intelligently check up on ourselves.

The effective Bible reader must give attention first to the control of his breath in speaking. Breath is the material for tone, and its use must be regulated by the proper musculature. The upper torso, or rib cage, contains the lungs, which receive air on inhalation. Speech is produced on the exhaled breath, and the regulation of exhalation is controlled largely by the diaphragmatic muscle that forms the floor of the rib cage.

Exhaled breath passing between the vocal bands, which are located in the larynx or voice box, sets them in vibration, and this produces tone. In turn, this tone must be amplified and resonated in the throat, the mouth, and the nose. The organs of articulation—the lips, teeth, tongue, and hard and soft palates—produce intelligible speech sounds that result in spoken language.

Faults in tone production that are common to the would-be Bible reader may be indicated as follows.

Faults in Tone Production

1. Infrequent breathing. Breathing for life is one thing. Here inhalation and exhalation are fairly regular. Breathing for speech is another matter. Here the speaker must inhale quickly and silently and exhale slowly while his speech organs are formulating intelligible sounds.

There is a tendency in untrained speakers to speak on and on until they run out of breath. A good rule for the beginning speaker is to breathe every chance he has. We speak in phrases or word group patterns, usually not more than seven words in length. They cluster about a central thought that is indispensable to the meaning. Pauses between these phrases or word groups offer one opportunity to take a breath. The experienced speaker may have developed such good control that he can speak more than one related phrase in a breath. But a beginning speaker should take the opportunity to renew his breath supply so that his discourse always has adequate breath support. This will avoid the tendency to drop the volume on the ends of phrases, where the most important word often is, because one has too little breath support left. And it is true that infrequent breathing on the part even of experienced speakers can put unnecessary strain on the vocal bands and eventually cause a serious voice problem.

ARE YOU BREATHING OFTEN ENOUGH?

Long pauses allow the reader to take in a new and deep breath. Short pauses allow one to take in a small amount of breath so that there is always support for the words yet to be spoken on the phrase or idea.

The following exercise should help the inexperienced speaker to develop good breath control. Practice will eliminate any temporary jerkiness in speaking as one masters the art of regulated breathing. And keep your mind alert. Body and mind work together.

The diagonal slash (/) indicates opportunity to take a full breath. The check mark (✔) indicates an opportunity to supplement the breath already in the lungs to fully support the next phrase. Voice the following, breathing as indicated:

Make a joyful noise unto the Lord, ✔ all ye lands./

Serve the Lord with gladness:/
Come before his presence ✔ with singing./

Know ye ✔ that the Lord ✔ he is God:/
It is he that hath made us, ✔
And not we ourselves;/
We are his people, ✔ and the sheep of his pasture./

Enter into his gates ✔ with thanksgiving,/
And into his courts ✔ with praise:/
Be thankful unto him, ✔ and bless his name./

For the Lord is good;/
His mercy is everlasting;/
And his truth endureth to all generations/ *(Psalm 100)*.

2. Another common fault is throaty constriction. This is a tightening either of the muscles that control phonation or of the musculature that sheathes the back side of the pharynx or throat. Tension here can cause pain and also prevent the full, rich resonation of the note that is required for adequate vocal expression. Work upon such passages as the following should help to relieve tension and aid in producing clear, pure tone.

Bless the Lord, O my soul:
And all that is within me,
Bless his holy name *(Ps. 103:1)*.

> Come unto me, all ye that labour and are heavy laden,
> And I will give you rest *(Matt. 11:28)*.
>
> Peace I leave with you, my peace I give unto you:
> Not as the world giveth, give I unto you.
> Let not your heart be troubled,
> Neither let it be afraid *(John 14:27)*.

Open your mouth wide; breathe deeply; feel full relaxation of the throat.

3. A third fault that will affect adversely the effort to read the Bible well in public concerns proper *articulation*. Tone is shaped into intelligible speech by the tongue, the teeth, the lips, and the hard and soft palates. These sounds in any language must be learned with their meanings, and we learn to talk or communicate at a very early age. But carelessness, imitation of others, inattention, and the acquirement of bad speaking habits often result in mumbled, slurred, or sloppy articulation. Failure to get the mouth open and speaking at a rapid rate contribute to the problem. Family and friends become accustomed to our poor diction, and we are unaware of our failure to speak clearly and intelligibly.

Not only must articulation be distinct and pleasing, it must be accurate. This involves the proper *pronunciation* of words. Pronunciation concerns the particular sound given to vowels and consonants in any given word. It is determined arbitrarily and is recorded in a standard dictionary. Accent upon certain syllables is also involved. The accepted pronunciation for biblical proper names is available in a biblical dictionary. To still mispronounce words in reading any passage, after time for preparation has been given, is inexcusable. Do not attempt to read any word whose meaning is unclear to you and which you cannot accurately pronounce. Attention to this phase of your improvement is essential.

This is not a new idea! Back in the days of Nehemiah the prophet, when the people gathered together to hear the priests read the Word of God from handwritten scrolls, we have this enlightening comment: "So they read in the book in the law of God *distinctly*, and gave the sense, and caused them to *understand* the reading" (Neh. 8:8, italics added).

Careful reading of a passage such as James 3:3-5 should make a speaker conscious of the accuracy of his enunciation.

> Behold, we put bits in the horses' mouths, that they may obey us; and we turn about their whole body.
>
> Behold also the ships, which though they be so great, and are driven of fierce winds, yet are they turned about with a very small helm, whithersoever the governor listeth.
>
> Even so the tongue is a little member, and boasteth great things. Behold, how great a matter a little fire kindleth!

There are many and varied faults of voice. Perhaps calling attention to these few basic problems will alert the reader to listen to his own voice, to analyze his particular needs, and to seek improvement through cultivation of right habits of tone production. Better yet, seek out a competent judge of the human voice and get an evaluation of the use of your own.

Expressive Actions of the Voice

We must be aware of the tools we have to express thinking and feeling and to use intelligently in reading the Scriptures.

First, we are capable of changing *pitch*. The voice has a range from low to high, and as we speak, the melody of our voices and the tune they sing convey meaning.

We may change pitch between words and phrases. This shows discrimination and is the chief element in subordination, for we tend to put on a lower pitch that which is less important.

CHANGE OF PITCH

We may also change pitch *upon* a word on its accented syllable, going from low to high or from high to low. This change is called inflection.

Length of inflection reveals the importance of the word. Direction of inflection reveals the degree of completeness of the idea that the word expresses. A rising inflection indicates more to follow, a question or surprise. A falling inflection indicates certainty, assurance, finality.

A certain man had two sons *(Luke 15:11).*

Man receives a longer inflection than either *a* or *certain* because it is more important. *Sons* also receives a longer inflection than either *had* or *two*. The direction of inflection of *man* is rising because the thought is not yet complete. *Sons* has a falling inflection because this completes the entire idea.

It is especially important for one who wishes to read the Bible well to cultivate a wide and expressive range of pitches. So common has been the tendency of ministers to repeat the same patterns of pitches that this fault has been given a name. It is called "ministerial tune." It has no place in effective reading of the Word.

Equally distressing is a tendency of some ministers to let their firm touch upon an inflected word slip, thus causing the inflection to go in two directions. This circumflex inflection is the true language of joke, sarcasm, or insincerity. Such inflection sounds affected in the serious reading of God's Word and should be avoided. I fear it is sometimes even cultivated in the mistaken hope of appearing to be well trained.

RATE A second expressive action of the voice is *rate*. Rate denotes the mode of progression of the thought. It may be slow or rapid, light or heavy, measured or quick, or a combination of these. It is more than tempo. Rate reveals the inherent character of a passage or a person.

Contrast the changes in rate or movement between the words of the Samaritan woman and Jesus Christ as recorded in John 4:11-14. In the beginning of the narrative she is curious, superficial, self-defensive.

> Sir, thou hast nothing to draw with, and the well is deep: from whence then hast thou that living water?

A light, rapid, uneven rate will reveal her spirit. Note the assurance, the penetration, the confidence of the Master as He replies,

> Whosoever drinketh of the water that I shall give him shall never thirst; but the water that I shall give him shall be in him a well of water springing up into everlasting life.

The rate here would be strong, slow, and with a definite regular pulsation.

A third expressive action of the voice is *quality*. This is the language of the emotions, and it is heard in varying kinds of resonance or timbre. To read the Bible without expressing feelings is to render it cold and mechanical and without personal application.

QUALITY

An effort to express by the voice varying emotions will give the reader an awareness of his own vocal quality and will assist him in making it more evident. This is not an affectation. It comes from genuine realization of the emotion inherent in the words of any given passage.

Chosen passages from the account of the walk to Emmaus as recorded in Luke 24:13-35 register varying emotions.

> What manner of communications are these that ye have one to another, as ye walk, and are sad? (The interested Lord)
>
> We trusted that it had been he which should have redeemed Israel. (The disillusioned disciples)
>
> O fools, and slow of heart to believe all that the prophets have spoken. (The compassionate Jesus)
>
> Abide with us. (The imploring disciples)
>
> Their eyes were opened, and they knew him. (The sympathetic and joyous narrators)

Did not our heart burn within us, while he talked with us by the way . . . ? (The transformed disciples)

The Lord is risen indeed. (The triumphant witnesses)

He was known of them in breaking of bread. (The participating spectators)

There is another expressive action of the voice, very valuable and necessary in interpreting Scripture. This is the *pause*. A pause is a period of silence preceding an idea, during which both the speaker and the hearers are preparing for the expression of that idea. Its length is proportionate to the importance of the idea or its emotional content or to the passage or time it might denote.

PAUSE A period of silence for emphasis may also occur either preceding or following the idea to which it relates. This silence is an effective way of commanding attention. It actually says, "Hush!" "Hear!"

Marks of punctuation aid in setting words into phrase groups and in indicating where and how long should be the pauses that separate them. But they are not an infallible guide. The understanding of a passage is the surest dictator of the effective and natural use of the pause.

Study of a passage such as that recorded in Acts 7:54-60, which recounts the death of Stephen, the first Christian martyr, illustrates the progressive and dramatic use of pauses—these meaningful periods of silence that punctuate all thoughtful and gripping discourse.

54 When they [the mob] heard these things [Stephen's accusations against their hypocrisies], they were cut to the heart, and they gnashed on him with their teeth.

55 But he, being full of the Holy Ghost, looked up stedfastly into heaven, and saw the glory of God, and Jesus standing on the right hand of God,   56 And said, Behold, I see the heavens opened, and the Son of man standing on the right hand of God.

57 Then they cried out with a loud voice, and stopped their ears, and ran upon him with one accord, 58 And cast him out of the city, and stoned him: and the witnesses laid down their clothes at a young man's feet, whose name was Saul.

59 And they stoned Stephen, calling upon God, and saying, Lord Jesus, receive my spirit.

60 And he kneeled down, and cried with a loud voice, Lord, lay not this sin to their charge. And when he had said this, he fell asleep.

The pauses that occur in reading the reactions of the angry, violent mob are abrupt and emotion-packed (vv. 54, 57). Those that reveal the calm, radiant spirit of Stephen are longer and stronger (vv. 55, 60). Those emphatic pauses that follow the words *Jesus* (v. 55), *Son of man* (v. 56), and *Lord Jesus* (v. 59) actually give the listeners time to see the vision of Christ that is captivating and sustaining the noble Stephen, who sees Him standing at the right hand of God.

Many have noted that in every other place in the Bible where the resurrected Christ is mentioned, He is described as sitting at the Father's side; but here He is recorded as "standing" as with a rising ovation He welcomes the martyr Stephen.

Another strong, emphatic pause follows "and stoned him" (v. 58). And there is a long pause following his words "Lord, lay not this sin to their charge." It is an echo from Calvary and partakes of the spirit of the Master himself who, as He died, cried, "Father, forgive them; for they know not what they do" (Luke 23:34).

There is still another expressive action of the voice. This is the proper use of *force* or *volume.* It is regulated by the supply of breath. It should vary with the degree of importance of the idea expressed.

FORCE It is first evidenced in the accent or greater ictus upon syllables. This is an arbitrary and predetermined thing. Then it is heard in the reception of greater force upon the central word of a phrase. Finally, use of force is demonstrated by the greater amount of volume employed in expressing a whole sentence or even a paragraph.

There is perfect harmony between the use of pitch and the use of volume. The word receiving the longest inflection in a phrase will always be the word to receive the greatest amount of force because it is the indispensable word in that grouping. Likewise, the subordinate words receiving minor pitch changes will also be the words receiving less volume.

An examination of a familiar passage such as Psalm 23 will indicate the words in each phrase group that should receive the greater volume or ictus. They are the central words. They tell the story. They are here underlined to indicate that they receive the greater force.

> The <u>Lord</u> is my <u>shepherd</u>; I shall <u>not want</u>.
> He maketh me to lie down in <u>green pastures</u>:
> He leadeth me beside the <u>still waters</u>.
> He <u>restoreth</u> my <u>soul</u>:
>
> He leadeth me in the paths of <u>righteousness</u>
> For his <u>name's sake</u>.
> <u>Yea</u>, though I walk through the valley of the shadow of <u>death</u>,
> I will fear <u>no evil</u>:
> For <u>thou</u> art <u>with me</u>;
> Thy <u>rod</u> and thy <u>staff</u> they <u>comfort</u> me.
>
> Thou preparest a <u>table</u> before me
> In the presence of mine <u>enemies</u>:
> Thou anointest my <u>head</u> with <u>oil</u>;
> My <u>cup runneth over</u>.
>
> Surely <u>goodness</u> and <u>mercy</u> shall follow me
> All the <u>days of my life</u>:
> And I will dwell in the <u>house of the Lord for ever</u>.

In discussing volume as an expressive action of the voice, it should also be noted that the amount of force used throughout a reading depends upon the size of the audience and their proximity to the speaker. It is a primary law that unless one is heard, there is no use in his speaking. Tone must be projected so that the hearers listen in comfort and without strain. The speaker's voice must get "out." Furthermore, no voice can be made expressive and meaningful unless it has sufficient volume to be useful. You cannot paint a picture without any paint. Breath is the material for tone, and tone is the material for speech.

The effective speaker will take a new breath at every opportunity. Thus he never runs out of breath and is able to project his voice with firmness and authority.

Examination of a passage in an effort to unite all these expressive modulations of the voice will hopefully show that they work harmoniously and interchangeably to convey meaning.

In Matt. 7:24-27, we have recorded the parable of the two houses, one built upon the rock and the other on the sand.

> Therefore whosoever heareth these sayings of mine, and doeth them, I will liken him unto a wise man, which built his house upon a rock.

The three indispensable words in this verse are *doeth, wise,* and *rock*. They will receive the longest inflections, which will, in all cases, be falling; and they will also receive the greater degree of force. *Man* and *house* receive lesser degrees of emphasis, as they support the central words. The rate of speaking the introductory clause will be light and rapid.

> And the rain descended, and the floods came, and the winds blew, and beat upon that house; and it fell not: for it was founded upon a rock.

The rate in reading the description of the storm will be rapid and heavy to denote the intensity of the attack. The inflections of the words *descended, came, blew, beat,* and *house* will continue to be rising to indicate that the fury of the storm is continuous and is not spent until we realize that the house stands! *It fell not! Not* is the important word and receives both strong volume and a falling inflection. The description of the storm will also bring out color in the quality of the voice, and there will be a note of triumph and rejoicing that the house stood.

> And every one that heareth these sayings of mine, and doeth them not, shall be likened unto a foolish man, which built his house upon the sand:
>
> And the rain descended, and the floods came, and the winds blew, and beat upon that house; and it fell: and great was the fall of it.

Likewise, the second half of the parable moves rapidly since the material is already familiar, until we come to the word *not* with the words *foolish* and *sand* receiving both volume and a falling inflection. The pronoun *his* may receive antithetical inflection to further differentiate this man from the first.

It is the very same storm. It should be read with the same intense and rapid rate. But the shock comes with the word *fell*, given with a strong falling inflection followed by an emphatic pause. The last clause is spoken with finality and regret coloring the voice.

Try it aloud! That is the only way you will ever become a true interpreter of the Word of God.

The voice is the speaker's instrument for declaring the sublimest thoughts ever to be penned. What care we should use in producing it and reducing it to intelligible speech! What cultivation we should give to the expressive actions of the voice until they become our responsive medium for interpreting to mankind the very thoughts of God!

A GLORIOUS INSTRUMENT—THE HUMAN VOICE

Since we are considering the oral interpretation of the Scriptures, it should prove profitable to keep ever before us that the Word was indeed first spoken by the human voice and that it is preeminently fitted to be delivered orally.

The Voices of the Storytellers

Now let us consider these historical men and women who actually did speak the words of God. They adopted various literary forms perhaps unconsciously because these mediums best expressed the messages they had to deliver.

First came the storytellers.

A story or narrative is one of the most natural and spontaneous means of communication. It has appeal for both the speaker and the hearer. Its telling is motivated by a desire to share, to inform, to entertain, to interest. It consists of a series of related events moving in sequence toward a climax. It is peopled by characters. It is sustained by a plot. It seeks a response, which is indirect but nonetheless important to the success of the telling.

The hearer at its completion should register pleasure, approval, joy, regret, or disappointment. The story is not a soliloquy. It is justified only because it is heard and has elicited a response.

POWERFUL MEDIUM—THE STORY

The story always has a setting—a place in time and space where the action occurs. It is a happening. It involves persons in interaction in relation to one another. Character is revealed. But the story is not a biography. It is dominated by action, and any dialogue introduced is there to contribute to the movement of the story.

There is a very real sense in which all biblical narratives have a dramatic element, for people are always involved. We are concerned with their character traits, their attitudes, their strengths or weaknesses, their reactions to other people, their development, their ultimate triumph or defeat as revealed in the climax of the story.

There is in human nature a tendency to "other" oneself. We do this with what we see or hear or read about. We tend to re-create scenes and situations, to relive experiences, to see things from another's viewpoint, to participate sympathetically in the joys and sorrows, the successes and the failures of other human beings. Though personalities differ in the degree to which they can respond to these things, everyone possesses some ability to ally himself with another, unless these instincts and impulses have been stifled and inhibited until the spontaneous response is weak or lacking altogether.

So as an oral interpreter, to read a Bible narrative well, we must allow this dramatic tendency to function. There will not be an impersonation of the characters involved, but there will be an interpretation of them. Our voices will suggest their pleasure, resentment, anger, amazement, duplicity, impatience, gratitude, or whatever emotion dominates them for the moment. The intrinsic musculature of the body will respond to these varying states of mind and feeling. There will be a minimum of physical movement; there will be a full reaction in the conditional response of the body.

The oral reader becomes the storyteller. He is involved. He presents viewpoints, he participates in the action, he is glad or sad at the results. He takes sides; he attempts to faithfully represent each angle of the conflict whether or not he agrees personally with that point of view.

The storyteller must have a clear sense of the progression of the story. It is often chronological, but this is more than a mere time sequence. There is the development of plot, the reaction and development of characters, the intensifying of interest, the resolution of the dilemma. There is a point in a well-narrated story. When it has been made, it is left with the hearer. He is not pressed for a verdict.

IT MUST BE RELIVED

Progression is sometimes achieved through description as events move forward toward the climax. Again dialogue or conversation between characters advances the story.

Bible narratives vary in length, but all have certain common characteristics. They are not cluttered with verbiage; they are not burdened with detail. Their language is simple and direct. They leave much to the imagination. They are swift moving. The climax is the high point of the narrative, and very few words are needed as a conclusion following the climax.

In reading a Bible narrative, opening sentences are highly important, for they give the location of the action about to be recounted and perhaps even introduce the characters involved, which must always be done with clarity and distinction. Transitions from one event to another must be carefully marked by the voice, since they indicate the progressions of the story.

A transition is indicated by a pause, a change of pitch, and often a change of rate. The climax of the story must have its most telling vocal expression—longer pauses, stronger inflections, and intensification of both rate and color.

Practice in the oral reading of the narrative form is a good place to begin this project of improved Bible reading.

The Historians

Among Bible narratives, we note first those that recount events that have taken place. They are of such significance as to deserve perpetuation. One is impressed at once by the fact that Bible narratives are unequivocally faithful to truth.

Nothing is shaded, no evidence is withheld. They are the essence of reality.

This gives to them a stark and rugged grandeur that unfailingly challenges the reader to be as honest and as faithful in re-creating them as was their author in first transcribing them. This is why no matter how familiar they may be, their reliving rewards the reader with some new strength, some unseen beauty. Let no reader of a Bible narrative offer the excuse, "That's familiar. The audience has heard that!" No! Therein lies our greatest challenge: to bring forth "things new and old" from the Word (Matt. 13:52).

A WELL-TOLD STORY NEVER GROWS OLD

I love to tell the story; 'Tis pleasant to repeat
What seems each time I tell it More wonderfully sweet.
—KATHERINE HANKEY

The historical narratives of the Bible abound in the Old Testament: the stories of creation; of the Flood; of Abraham, Isaac, and Jacob; of Joseph, Gideon, Samson, and Samuel; of Ruth and Esther and David.

The stories of the four Gospels in the New Testament and of the Acts of the Apostles are all examples of historical narratives. They offer the public Scripture reader an exhaustless supply of incomparable material.

One of the most perfect examples of such a narrative is found in Gen. 22:1-14.

It is well for the reader to determine the point or impact of the story he is about to relate even though this title or purpose may not be shared with the audience. This narrative might be titled "Abraham's Test of Faith" or "God Tests Abraham."

> 1 God did tempt [tested] Abraham, and said unto him, Abraham: and he said, Behold, here I am. ["Tempt" is here better translated "test." God does not tempt men.]

> 2 And he said, Take now thy son, thine only son Isaac, whom thou lovest, and get thee into the land of Moriah; and offer him there for a burnt offering upon one of the mountains which I will tell thee of.

This seems a shocking request, and it was. But the offering of human sacrifice in that dark era of history was practiced by heathen religions and would not have been unfamiliar to Abraham.

We must realize that though the night may have been a sleepless one, Abraham's obedience the following day was implicit and unhesitating. The voice will carry the promptness with which Abraham followed God's instructions. There was no "Well, now, Lord, it seems to me that is a perfectly illogical request"; or "I am not sure I heard You aright, Lord." On the contrary,

> 3 And Abraham rose up early in the morning, and saddled his ass, and took two of his young men with him, and Isaac his son, and clave the wood for the burnt offering, and rose up, and went unto the place of which God had told him.
>
> 4 Then on the third day Abraham lifted up his eyes, and saw the place afar off.
>
> 5 And Abraham said unto his young men, Abide ye here with the ass; and I and the lad will go yonder and worship, and come again to you.

The voice of the reader must show Abraham's sublime faith shining through: *We will "come again to you"!*

> 6 And Abraham took the wood of the burnt offering, and laid it upon Isaac his son; and he took the fire in his hand, and a knife; and they went both of them together.

Such fortitude! Such strength! How tall the man stood!

> 7 And Isaac spake unto Abraham his father, and said, My father: and he said, Here am I, my son.

Always the same confident reply, "Here I am." In the path of perfect obedience! Where else?

> And he said, Behold the fire and the wood: but where is the lamb for a burnt offering?
>
> 8 And Abraham said, My son, God will provide himself a lamb for a burnt offering: so they went both of them together.

Remember, Isaac may not have been a child, though he is referred to as a "lad." He was probably a young man of 20 or more years. His inquiry was understandable, but his acceptance of his father's answer was amazing. He, too, shares in his father's spirit of total submission to God. He reminds us of that One who, facing death, bowed His head in submission to the Father and prayed, "Not my will, but thine, be done" (Luke 22:42).

DO YOU IDENTIFY?

> 9 And they came to the place which God had told him of; and Abraham built an altar there, and laid the wood in order, and bound Isaac his son, and laid him on the altar upon the wood.

The deliberate, methodical rate begins to quicken.

> 10 And Abraham stretched forth his hand, and took the knife to slay his son.

And now it seems God was in haste to stop the patriarch, intent upon obedience, even when it involved slaying his own son. "Abraham, Abraham!" Abrupt! Urgent!

> 11 And the angel of the Lord called unto him out of heaven, and said, Abraham, Abraham: and he said, Here am I.

Note his answer—"Here am I." (The same as before.)

> 12 And he said, Lay not thine hand upon the lad, neither do thou any thing unto him: for now I know that thou fearest God, seeing thou hast not withheld thy son, thine only son from me.

Perfect approval!

> 13 And Abraham lifted up his eyes, and looked, and behold behind him a ram caught in a thicket by his horns: and Abra-

ham went and took the ram, and offered him up for a burnt offering in the stead of his son.

Isn't it a commentary on our faithless, insensitive lives that as soon as we hear God calling us to some mount of sacrifice to turn over to Him our dearest possession, we begin beating the bushes to find the ram! Surely there must be an alternative to the path of perfect obedience! Abraham's implicit faith shames our faithlessness! And do not anticipate the ram!

14 And Abraham called the name of that place Jehovah-jireh: as it is said to this day, In the mount of the Lord it shall be seen.

Other historical narratives from the Old Testament that will afford rewarding oral practice are:

        The Creation—Genesis 1 and 2
        The Temptation and Fall of Man—Genesis 3
        The Foretelling of the Destruction of Sodom—Genesis 18
        The Destruction of Sodom—Gen. 19:1-29
        Abraham's Servant's Journey to Find Rebekah—Genesis 24
        Esau Selling His Birthright—Gen. 25:27-34
        Deception of Isaac by Jacob and Rebekah—Genesis 27
        Jacob and the Vision of Angels—Genesis 28
        Jacob Wrestling at Peniel—Genesis 32
        The Selling of Joseph to the Midianites—Genesis 37
        Joseph's Reconciliation with His Brothers—Genesis 45
        The Rescue of the Baby Moses—Exod. 2:1-10
        The Death of Samson—Judg. 16:4-31
        The Book of Ruth
        Samuel Called of the Lord—1 Samuel 3
        David and Goliath Meet—1 Sam. 17:1-51

David Mourns Absalom's Death—2 Sam. 18:18-33
God's Care of Elijah—1 Kings 17
The Contest on Mount Carmel—1 Kings 18:17-40
The Widow's Oil Multiplied—2 Kings 4:1-7
The Story of the Shunammite Woman—2 Kings 4:8-37
The Healing of Naaman the Leper—2 Kings 5
Rebuilding the Temple—Nehemiah 4
The Book of Esther
The Hebrew Children in the Fiery Furnace—Daniel 3
Belshazzar's Feast—Daniel 5
Daniel in the Lions' Den—Daniel 6

The historical narratives of the New Testament are similar to those of the Old Testament: direct, unadorned, utterly true. There is one small distinction that really should not make a difference. In the Old Testament, God the Almighty speaks. His voice is authoritative, commanding, yet compassionate. In the New Testament, the Word has been made flesh, and we are interpreting the voice of Jesus, the Godman, still almighty, yet touched with the deep sense of human need. They are one; yet in the Son we have a revelation of the Father that reaches to our inmost being. To attempt to interpret the voices of both will challenge the best of our capacities. In Jesus' voice we must suggest tenderness, compassion, understanding.

The miracles of Jesus offer material for such a study. A favorite is found in John 6:5-14. It might be titled "The Messiah Has Come" or "This Is the Messiah."

A narrative always happens in a setting.

3 Jesus went up into a mountain, and there he sat with his disciples.

Here it is in the rolling Galilean hills; there is green grass; there are fluffy white clouds in the azure sky. Jesus and the Twelve are seated on the ground for a moment of rest.

And now the action starts:

> 5 When Jesus then lifted up his eyes, and saw a great company come unto him, he saith unto Philip, Whence shall we buy bread, that these may eat?

He is aware of elemental human need. They're hungry! He approaches Philip, the practical one. "Do you have any ideas?"

> 6 And this he said to prove him: for he himself knew what he would do.

Parenthetical—spoken in a low tone, almost a whisper. But how reassuring to us when we are about to panic in a set of overwhelming circumstances. He knows what to do.

> 7 Philip answered him, Two hundred pennyworth of bread is not sufficient for them, that every one of them may take a little.

The pragmatist, figuring it all out at the end of his pencil. Still no solution.

> 8 One of his disciples, Andrew, Simon Peter's brother, saith unto him,
>
> 9 There is a lad here, which hath five barley loaves, and two small fishes: but what are they among so many?

Dear Andrew, the people person, still having to use his brother Simon for identification, has been out in the crowd, making friends, and has found the material for a miracle but doesn't recognize it. Still baffled by the milling crowd. *So many!*

> 10 And Jesus said, Make the men sit down.

The Master takes over—His voice not arrogant nor peremptory, not cocky nor self-assured. Capable, confident, all-powerful, the Mighty God, yet the tender, loving Savior, knowing what it meant to be hungry and weary.

> Now there was much grass in the place. So the men sat down, in number about five thousand.

> 11 And Jesus took the loaves; and when he had given thanks, he distributed to the disciples, and the disciples to them that were set down; and likewise of the fishes as much as they would.

When He had given thanks—what a beautiful reminder to us that every gift is from above, even the daily necessities of life, and they should always be accepted with expressed gratitude.

> 12 When they were filled,

Never meager, always an abundance—

> he said unto his disciples, Gather up the fragments that remain, that nothing be lost.

Another lesson in conservation so needed in our wasteful, indulgent, prodigal day.

> 13 Therefore they gathered them together, and filled twelve baskets with the fragments of the five barley loaves, which remained over and above unto them that had eaten.

A basketful for each disciple! And yet this isn't the miracle! Don't get so overwhelmed with what was *left* that you fail to convince us that 5,000 men, besides women and children, were filled to satiety.

> 14 Then those men, when they had seen the miracle that Jesus did, said, This is of a truth that prophet that should come into the world.

This is not just a concluding statement. This is the biggest line of all, the realization of His Messiahship. *This is He!* And who could have felt it more than the little lad whose lunch He borrowed. And that mother back home who had packed the lunch, when she heard the wonder, she, too, must have believed. Get them all in—more than 5,000 of them. *"This is of a truth that prophet that should come into the world!"*

MAKE IT BIG!

Other very readable historical narratives in the New Testament are:

> The Birth of Jesus—Matt. 2:1-12; Luke 2:1-20
> The Baptism of Jesus—Matthew 3
> The Temptation of Jesus—Matt. 4:1-11
> The Storm on Galilee—Matt. 8:23-27
> Peter Walks on the Water—Matt. 14:22-33
> The Transfiguration—Matt. 17:1-9
> The Last Supper—Matt. 26:17-30
> Gethsemane and the Taking of Jesus—Matt. 26:36-56
> Healing of the Lame Man—Mark 2:1-12
> Healing of the Woman Ill for 12 Years—Mark 5:25-34
> The Triumphal Entry into Jerusalem—Mark 11:1-11
> Healing of the Centurion's Servant—Luke 7:1-10
> Jesus in the House of Simon—Luke 7:36-50
> The Story of Zacchaeus—Luke 19:1-10
> The Walk to Emmaus—Luke 24:13-35
> Marriage in Cana of Galilee—John 2:1-10
> Jesus and the Woman of Samaria—John 4:4-42
> Healing of the Blind Man—John 9:1-38
> Raising of Lazarus—John 11:1-46
> Washing the Disciples' Feet—John 13:1-17
> Resurrection Morning—John 20:1-18
> Breakfast on the Shore—John 21:1-19
> Healing of the Lame Man—Acts 3:1-11
> Ananias and Sapphira—Acts 5:1-11
> Saul on the Damascus Road—Acts 9:1-19
> Deliverance from the Philippian Jail—Acts 16:16-40

The Users of Parables

There is another distinct type of Bible narrative that deserves special attention. This is the parable. Now it is certainly true that from all Bible narratives one may derive certain lessons. They all embody and enliven applicable truth. They reveal moral and spiritual values.

But the parable form is expressly designed to do this. Under cover of its story form, it conceals a hidden meaning, and this is why it is told. It is not the recounting of an actual happening, and though it is never untrue to life, it is not actually a "true story." Because its meaning is veiled, it is rendered acceptable to those who might reject this meaning if it were expressly stated. It is an art form especially used by the Master but evident in all Scripture. It is a colorful means of making abstract truth concrete.

The parable is always brief, and because it is single-minded, it should not be expected to "walk on all fours" or have significance in every detail. Sometimes the parables of the Bible are analyzed or explained. More often they are left for the hearer to interpret for himself.

The parabolic spirit is seen not only in the complete narrative form that is familiar to all students of the Word, but also in the metaphors and similes that abound throughout the Scriptures. Think of the figurative language used to describe the Son of God. He is

The Rose of Sharon
   The Lily of the Valley
      The Bright and Morning Star
         The Lamb of God
            The Lion of the Tribe of Judah
               King of Kings
                  Alpha and Omega—The Beginning and the End
                     The Bread Sent Down from Heaven
                     The Water of Life
                        A Rock in a Weary Land

The rich imagery found in the Book of Proverbs and the Psalms partakes of the parabolic spirit. It abounds in the words of the prophets.

> The Lord is my rock, and my fortress, . . . my buckler, and the horn of my salvation, and my high tower *(Ps. 18:2)*.
>
> All we like sheep have gone astray *(Isa. 53:6)*.
>
> Though your sins be as scarlet, they shall be as white as snow; though they be red like crimson, they shall be as wool *(Isa. 1:18)*.

To properly interpret these beautiful figures with their suggested meaning requires an imaginative approach. They are dead if they are read factually. A mental picturing of the image portrayed will give color and richness to the voice.

And why should we be wary of using the imagination? It has been repudiated as mere fancy, unreality, and has even been maligned as an affectation. This is so wrong. Imagination is a God-given faculty of the mind whereby we can create a situation or an event and thus relate ourselves to it and become a participant in it. We can make it all happen again. Without imagination it is impossible to "other" ourselves. We live in the cramped and egocentric world of our own experience. Imagination widens our horizons and broadens our perspectives. But because we are bound by bad habits or a false conventionality, or because we are fearful of being called "phony" or "overdone," we clamp our expression in a vice, and it comes out dead and stereotyped, without ability to stir ourselves or anyone else. To effectively read the parable form, or in fact any narrative, one must first allow his imagination to create the image or the situation set forth; then by his voice he can depict the hidden meaning with beauty and truth.

**RECREATE!
USE IMAGINATION!**

The parabolic narrative is used to make vivid and pointed a hidden truth. Through the progression of events and the actions and reactions of characters, the story moves to its climax. The reader must always have in mind the underlying meaning. This conscious projection of that which is only implied will lengthen the pauses, make the inflections longer and stronger, and sharpen the discriminative actions of the mind as revealed in wide changes of pitch and variations in rate.

A noble example of the parable is found in Luke 10:25-37 in the story familiarly called "The Good Samaritan." It might be titled "Who Is My Neighbor?"

The setting gives a perfect occasion for the use of the parable form. Here is Jesus, in the midst of His disciples, suddenly and acutely aware that these unlearned fishermen and tax collectors have an insight into spiritual matters that even the doctors of the law, the scribes, and the Pharisees did not enjoy. The mysteries of the Kingdom are hidden from the "wise and prudent" and have been "revealed . . . unto babes" (Matt. 11:25; Luke 10:21).

In the midst of the exalted contemplation, a lawyer, one of the "wise and prudent," seeking to trap Jesus, began to interrogate Him.

> 25 And, behold, a certain lawyer stood up, and tempted him, saying, Master, what shall I do to inherit eternal life?

It was not a sincere question. The voice can indicate this with circumflex inflections and a lack of real force.

Jesus counters with another question—a wise procedure.

> 26 He said unto him, What is written in the law? how readest thou?
>
> 27 And he answering said, Thou shalt love the Lord thy God with all thy heart, and with all thy soul, and with all thy strength, and with all thy mind; and thy neighbour as thyself.

The lawyer knows the law. He speaks it with assurance, and yet somehow he finds himself on the defensive.

28 And he said unto him, Thou hast answered right: this do, and thou shalt live.

Jesus, still in command, is ready to close the interview.

29 But he, willing to justify himself, said unto Jesus, And who is my neighbour?

We can almost forgive his nitpicking because it brings from the Master this marvelous revelation of divine truth. We, as well as the lawyer, need to hear it.

A parable is an illustration. It is a word picture of truth. It answers the question "Who is my neighbour?" better than any definition or analytical exegesis could do.

30 And Jesus answering said, A certain man went down from Jerusalem to Jericho, and fell among thieves, which stripped him of his raiment, and wounded him, and departed, leaving him half dead.

We do not know who this man was nor what his station in life was. That is not the point. Each mind, reader and hearer, will supply those details to make the picture vivid and realistic, but they are nonessential. We do know that the winding, mountainous road between Jerusalem and Jericho was beset by robbers who, hiding behind the great boulders that lined the road in places, could leap out and pounce upon a lonely traveler. He must have put up resistance. Before he had been relieved of his valuables and even of his clothing, he was so badly wounded that he was left half dead by his attackers. It is a sudden, violent, unjustified act. Read it so it sounds that way. You, along with the victim, are outraged.

ARE YOU RELIVING IT?

And now the plot thickens. The ecclesiastical leaders of the day get into the act. "The church" becomes involved.

31 And by chance there came down a certain <u>priest</u> that way: and when he saw him, he passed by on the other side.

32 And likewise a <u>Levite</u>, when he was at the place, came and looked on him, and passed by on the other side.

The most significant words in these verses are "and when he saw him" and "came and looked on him." They should be read with great weight and seriousness. It was not ignorance that left these representatives of the synagogue unmoved. It was indifference, preoccupation, irresponsibility, egomania. We are reminded of James's words:

> If a brother or sister be naked, and destitute of daily food, and one of you say unto them, Depart in peace, be ye warmed and filled; notwithstanding ye give them not those things which are needful to the body; what doth it profit? *(James 2:15-16)*.

An anonymous author has written, "I was cold and hungry, and you organized a committee."

MAKE IT POINTED

With regret the reader's voice registers the unconcern that the stricken man has to this point received. The parable is beginning to take hold. We are beginning to read hidden meanings. We are starting to ask ourselves, "Lord, is it I?"

And now the scene changes. The rate quickens, the melody begins to sing, joy and relief color the voice.

> 33 But a certain Samaritan, as he journeyed, came where he was: and when he saw him, he had compassion on him,
>
> 34 And went to him, and bound up his wounds, pouring in oil and wine, and set him on his own beast, and brought him to an inn, and took care of him.
>
> 35 And on the morrow when he departed, he took out two pence, and gave them to the host, and said unto him, Take care of him; and whatsoever thou spendest more, when I come again, I will repay thee.

This is the ultimate! Jesus piles one fact upon another until we have a perfect description of extravagant, uncalculating love. A Samaritan stopping to show pity on a Jew! This is unthinkable! But he had compassion, he gave him first aid, and he lifted the stricken man to the back of his own donkey while he himself walked to the inn where he could be cared for more effectively. Then he not only paid the bill but gave a promissory note for any further care the stranger would require. Love is a spendthrift!

This is the parable form, and it is charged with hidden meaning.

Now it is Jesus' turn to press His questions.

> 36 Which now of these three, thinkest thou, was neighbour unto him that fell among the thieves?
>
> 37 And he said, He that shewed mercy on him. Then said Jesus unto him, Go, and do thou likewise.

Now! How well did you read it aloud?

The Dramatists

There is a third area of storytelling that demands its own special analysis. It is true that people are a part of every well-structured narrative. But there are some instances where people seem to dominate the field more than the events that are transpiring. There is little description. There is not much broad action. The story progresses by the interactions and responses of the *persons* involved, one to the other. It is people—responding, rejecting, loving, despising, accepting, ignoring, deceiving, receiving other people.

Since the dramatic element definitely dominates, the content requires a different delivery than either the historical or the parabolic forms of the narrative. Scene changes and time sequence are not so important. We are concerned with *characters*—what they think, how they speak, how they interrelate, how they are influenced by one another, how they change, maturing or degenerating as the narrative progresses. We are deeply involved with them, getting their point of view and reaching out emotionally to them. We faithfully attempt to depict them, not as an impersonator but as an empathetic spectator.

These dramatic narratives do not always have a happy ending. In that, they partake of the great tragedies of literature.

Such a dramatic narrative is recorded in Mark 10:17-22. It is often referred to as the story of the rich young ruler. It might appropriately be titled "The Price of Discipleship."

> 17 And when he [Jesus] was gone forth into the way, there came one running, and kneeled to him, and asked him, Good Master, what shall I do that I may inherit eternal life?

Enter actor number one. He was eager: He came running. He was respectful: He kneeled and addressed Jesus as "Good Master." He was questioning: "What shall I do?" He was serious: He was thinking about eternal life.

> 18 And Jesus said unto him, Why callest thou me good? there is none good but one, that is, God.

What was his immediate response? Apparent rebuke! But it also gives hidden directive—to God. And Jesus continues explicitly:

> 19 Thou knowest the commandments, Do not commit adultery, Do not kill, Do not steal, Do not bear false witness, Defraud not, Honour thy father and mother.

Jesus was informed and assured. There is no hesitancy. He knows the way to eternal life. And what is the young man's response?

> 20 And he answered and said unto him, Master, all these have I observed from my youth.

Still respectful, but still in the clear. Still unsatisfied. Matthew has him say, "What lack I yet?" (19:20).

Jesus' reaction is immediate and overwhelming. He recognizes in this young man a sincere inquirer, not a Pharisee hoping to catch Him, not a lawyer seeking to entangle Him, but an honest believer, aware of unfulfilled longings, seeking truth. He loved him. And Jesus probes to the quick of his need. You should feel the dramatic change as the Master puts His sensitive finger on the young ruler's specific lack. The rate slows, the pitch lowers, and the intensity deepens.

> 21 Then Jesus beholding him loved him, and said unto him, One thing thou lackest: go thy way, sell whatsoever thou hast, and give to the poor, and thou shalt have treasure in heaven: and come, take up the cross, and follow me.

He who declared, "I came down from heaven, not to do mine own will, but the will of him that sent me" (John 6:38), had the prescription. He knew the antidote. It is the same for any and all who would possess eternal life: *Sell, give, come, follow!* Four mighty verbs! Here is the whole story of perfect fulfillment in the will of God; it is the way of the cross, the way of complete self-abnegation.

What was the young ruler's reaction? Sadness! Grief! Departure!

> 22 And he was sad at that saying, and went away grieved: for he had great possessions.

Spoken with infinite regret. The drama closes with his exit. We have no assurance that he ever returned. Here is a narrative consumed entirely with characters. They do not move from the scene on the stony Judean highway. The story is told entirely in dialogue. But what a story it is! How definitely we relate to the young man who only hears, "Sell and give." How yearningly we identify with Jesus who has also said, "Come and follow." Total commitment? Yes, but companionship with the Son of God here and for all eternity! And the young man went away!

DO YOU KNOW THIS YOUNG MAN?

The Voices of the Teachers

Instruction is the purpose and accounts for much of the content of the Bible. Its material is an appeal to the intellect; it is logical and reasonable. To establish fact until it becomes accepted truth and then to build this truth into irrefutable argument and a convincing conclusion is the task of the instructor or teacher.

If as oral interpreters we are to properly convey the messages of the original authors, we must know what kind of men they were, and we must prepare our minds to deliver the instruction they so effectively set forth.

First, they were thoroughly aware of the truth they proclaimed. Here there is no fumbling, no contradiction of terms, no illogical deductions. Their message was illuminating to others because it was unmistakably clear to those who were giving the instruction. This gave to their utterances the note of authority and assurance. To read the great declarations of the Bible in a weak and faltering voice or in a questioning or hesitant manner is to destroy their vitality and leave the hearers unconvinced and the reader baffled.

PERHAPS THIS IS YOUR GIFT— TO TEACH

"This then is the message which we have heard of him, and declare unto you, that God is light, and in him is no darkness at all" (1 John 1:5). The light of God's truth has shined in the mind and heart of the reader. He is convinced and he is convincing.

And yet the speaker must also have the spirit of the true teacher, which is one of infinite patience. There must be no dogmatism, no bigotry, no "take it or leave it" attitude. The purpose of the dedicated teacher is to impart knowledge, and he is never satified until the good has been accomplished. In reading the Word of God, the speaker applies its admonitions to himself, thus making truth acceptable to all. He is the mouthpiece; he, with his listeners, is sitting at the feet of the great Teacher.

> He that loveth not knoweth not God; for God is love. In this was manifested the love of God toward us, because that God sent his only begotten Son into the world, that we might live through him.
>
> **THIS IS GREAT TRUTH! DON'T READ IT CASUALLY!**
>
> Herein is love, not that we loved God, but that he loved us, and sent his Son to be the propitiation for our sins. Beloved, if God so loved us, we ought also to love one another *(1 John 4:8-11)*.

While audience awareness is present in any effective communication, it is absolutely essential to the teacher. He must constantly be saying by manner and intonation, though silently, "Do I make myself clear?" "Do you understand?" "Are you with me?" Such an attitude on his part saves the rendition from becoming a soliloquy on the one hand, or dead reiteration of meaningless phrases on the other. It must be a communication. Eye contact with the listener is vitally important. The very purpose—to impart, to give light, to clarify—gives tone and point to the message for the reader, and he becomes engrossed, not in himself but in the communication process.

The Users of Proverbs

The teaching literature assumes a number of forms in the Bible. First, let us examine the Proverbs. The Hebrew word for proverb means a comparison, and by this device abstract truth is made concrete; that is, a familiar example is used to portray a recognized fact or truth.

> A continual dropping in a very rainy day and a contentious woman are alike *(Prov. 27:15).*

This is a proverb—a pithy sentence expressing in a few words an obvious truth.

Drip, drip, drip! What better describes a nagging woman's voice? This should not be read with judgment or vindictiveness. It is so true it could even provoke a reaction not of bitterness or reproach but of agreement with a truth so well expressed. Try,

AREN'T THEY DELIGHTFUL!

> Iron sharpeneth iron; so a man sharpeneth the countenance of his friend *(Prov. 27:17).*

A recognition of the universal stimulation of tried and true friendships.

> Better is a dinner of herbs where love is, than a stalled ox and hatred therewith *(Prov. 15:17).*

How true! Better to sit down to turnip greens served on a table surrounded by love than to have T-bone steaks in an atmosphere of resentment, bitterness, and strife!

These lovely affirmations prove to be rich reading, not for one's private meditations alone, but for communicating to an audience. Because of their structure, there is a definite tendency to monotony in the reading of the Proverbs—monotony in rate, in pause, and in pitch. This produces a singsong rendition. Guard against it. The secret is to personalize every idea.

The following verses from Proverbs 3 are especial favorites. Read them with the relish of personal experience and realization, not as a preachment. This is the voice of the teacher who seeks to awaken in his hearers his own thoughts and feelings.

> Trust in the Lord with all thine heart;
> and lean not unto thine own understanding.
>
> In all thy ways acknowledge him,
> and he shall direct thy paths. . . .
>
> Honour the Lord with thy substance,
> and with the firstfruits of all thine increase:
>
> So shall thy barns be filled with plenty,
> and thy presses shall burst out with new wine.
>
> My son, despise not the chastening of the Lord;
> neither be weary of his correction:
>
> For whom the Lord loveth he correcteth;
> even as a father the son in whom he delighteth.
>
> Happy is the man that findeth wisdom,
> and the man that getteth understanding. . . .
>
> Length of days is in her right hand;
> and in her left hand riches and honour.
>
> Her ways are ways of pleasantness,
> and all her paths are peace. . . .
>
> My son, let not them depart from thine eyes:
> keep sound wisdom and discretion: . . .
>
> Then shalt thou walk in thy way safely,
> and thy foot shall not stumble.
>
> When thou liest down, thou shalt not be afraid:
> yea, thou shalt lie down,
> and thy sleep shall be sweet *(Prov. 3:5-6, 9-13, 16-17, 21, 23-24)*.

The comparisons must be cut in sharply, and the applications made clear. This means that the pauses between new ideas will be pronounced, and the changes of pitch between ideas distinct.

The well-known and beautiful account of a noble woman is found in Prov. 31:10-31. Do not read it as a lump. Let each descriptive phrase be accompanied by a definite mental picture in a realistic setting.

> Who can find a virtuous woman?
> for her price is far above rubies.

The heart of her husband doth safely trust in her,
so that he shall have no need of spoil.

She will do him good and not evil
all the days of her life.

She seeketh wool, and flax,
and worketh willingly with her hands.

She is like the merchants' ships;
she bringeth her food from afar.

She riseth also while it is yet night,
and giveth meat to her household,
and a portion to her maidens.

She considereth a field, and buyeth it:
with the fruit of her hands she planteth a vineyard.

She girdeth her loins with strength,
and strengtheneth her arms.

She perceiveth that her merchandise is good:
her candle goeth not out by night.

She layeth her hands to the spindle,
and her hands hold the distaff.

She stretcheth out her hand to the poor;
yea, she reacheth forth her hands to the needy.

She is not afraid of the snow for her household:
for all her household are clothed with scarlet.

She maketh herself coverings of tapestry;
her clothing is silk and purple.

Her husband is known in the gates,
when he sitteth among the elders of the land.

She maketh fine linen, and selleth it;
and delivereth girdles unto the merchant.

Strength and honour are her clothing;
and she shall rejoice in time to come.

She openeth her mouth with wisdom;
and in her tongue is the law of kindness.

She looketh well to the ways of her household,
and eateth not the bread of idleness.

> Her children arise up, and call her blessed;
> her husband also, and he praiseth her.
>
> Many daughters have done virtuously,
> but thou excellest them all.
>
> Favour is deceitful, and beauty is vain:
> but a woman that feareth the Lord, she shall be praised.
>
> Give her of the fruit of her hands;
> and let her own works praise her in the gates.

The imagery is very pronounced. Be sure you read with a picture in mind.

> "He shall have no need of spoil"; that is, she is a good financial manager. She knows how to balance the budget.
> > "All her household are clothed with scarlet"; that is, she provides for their warmth and comfort.
> > > "She . . . eateth not the bread of idleness"; that is, she is not lazy. She tends to business.
> > > > "Thou excellest them all"; that is, you're the greatest!

Hidden behind their figurative language, the Proverbs can teach the Christian believer some of life's most pertinent truths. They also give warning to the sinner and the backslider. Let us use them as a great teaching tool. When effectively presented by the human voice, they are potent.

The Letter Writers

A second teaching form permeates the New Testament. The letters of Paul, Peter, John, James, and Jude are classic examples. Nowhere in all of literature does this form reach the perfection of utterance to be found in the Bible.

A letter is a most personal form of discourse. Men commit to letters thoughts that they might not voice orally. The language of a well-written letter rises to a plane of eloquence seldom found in ordinary conversation. Letters are treasured, read, and reread. They become objects of value and of authority. Letters sometimes bring us closer to the one who wrote them than actual contact may do, because in a letter the writer dares to bare his very soul.

Letters reveal the personality of the writer and are enlivened with allusions to persons and incidents that add interest. All of this is true of the letters found in the Bible. But they are more. Because they were inspired by the Holy Spirit, they become a vehicle for teaching the truth of God, the unchanging verities of the kingdom of heaven.

LETTER WRITING IS ALMOST A LOST ART

So in the familiar medium of a letter, some of the most gripping facts of God's Word are taught. And remember, the letters were written to be read orally to the churches. In our quest for proficiency in Bible reading, the Epistles come in for their full share of attention. They are, for the most part, given as by a teacher to his pupils with love and understanding and with an eagerness that they might hear and assimilate the truth. As the teacher's index finger points out to his hearers, his other three fingers point back to himself. He, too, is a learner.

We must be aware that the various voices of the Bible are used interchangeably. Sometimes the letter writer uses the story form to illustrate a truth, and again the letter writer may rise to a high plane where his voice actually becomes that of the prophet or preacher. Experience will enable the reader to move from one purpose in speaking to another with ease and with smoothness, always keeping true to the message the speaker had in mind to proclaim.

An example of the teaching form as found in a letter can be noted in Romans 5. You are instructing. You are giving forth the truth.

Dead unto Sin—Alive unto Jesus Christ

Being justified by faith, we have peace with God through our Lord Jesus Christ: by whom also we have access by faith into

IS THIS YOUR EXPERIENCE?

this grace wherein we stand, and rejoice in hope of the glory of God.

And not only so, but we glory in tribulations also; knowing that tribulation worketh patience; and patience, experience; and experience, hope: and hope maketh not ashamed; because the love of God is shed abroad in our hearts by the Holy Ghost which is given unto us.

For when we were yet without strength, in due time Christ died for the ungodly. For scarcely for a righteous man will one

MAKE IT YOUR TESTIMONY

die: yet peradventure for a good man some would even dare to die. But God commendeth his love toward us, in that, while we were yet sinners, Christ died for us. Much more then, being now justified by his blood, we shall be saved from wrath through him. For if, when we were enemies, we were reconciled to God by the death of his Son, much more, being reconciled, we shall be saved by his life. And not only so, but we also joy in God through our Lord Jesus Christ, by whom we have now received the atonement.

Wherefore, as by one man sin entered into the world, and death by sin; and so death passed upon all men, for that all have sinned: . . . Therefore as by the offence of one judgment came upon all men to condemnation; even so by the righteousness of one the free gift came upon all men unto justification of life. For as by one man's disobedience many were made sinners, so by the obedience of one shall many be made righteous. Moreover the law entered, that the offence might abound. But where sin abounded, grace did much more abound:

That as sin hath reigned unto death, even so might grace reign through righteousness unto eternal life by Jesus Christ our Lord *(Rom. 5:1-12, 18-21).*

In this passage from Romans 5, Paul begins with some forthright assertions that should be spoken with assurance, though not with bombast.

The teaching spirit is felt as he warns against yielding to temptation and promises us certain victory through our Lord

Jesus. He progresses to the marvelous truth that Christ died for us when we were unrighteous sinners. Amazing love!

But now, because we have availed ourselves of His atonement, we stand justified before Him. Note the contrasted words—offence, righteousness; condemnation, justification; disobedience, obedience; sinners, righteous; law, grace; sin, grace; death, righteousness.

These words must be given a strong antithetical emphasis, both with greater volume and by the use of long inflections.

The admonitions of Paul to Timothy, his son in the gospel, have special meaning for all who are called to preach. One example is found in 1 Tim. 4:12-16.

> Let no man despise thy youth; but be thou an example of the believers, in word, in conversation, in charity, in spirit, in faith, in purity.
>
> **LIVE WITH THIS PASSAGE, PREACHERS** Till I come, give attendance to reading, to exhortation, to doctrine.
>
> Neglect not the gift that is in thee, which was given thee by prophecy, with the laying on of the hands of the presbytery.
>
> Meditate upon these things; give thyself wholly to them; that thy profiting may appear to all.
>
> Take heed unto thyself, and unto the doctrine; continue in them: for in doing this thou shalt both save thyself, and them that hear thee.

The words must be spoken with firmness of conviction, but with a tender love that takes away all harshness.

Similar instructions are found in 1 Tim. 6:6-12. Oral practice of them will develop in the reader the voice of the teacher.

> But godliness with contentment is great gain.
>
> For we brought nothing into this world, and it is certain we can carry nothing out.
>
> And having food and raiment let us be therewith content.

But they that will be rich fall into temptation and a snare, and into many foolish and hurtful lusts, which drown men in destruction and perdition.

DOES YOUR VOICE CONVEY THE TEACHING SPIRIT?

For the love of money is the root of all evil: which while some coveted after, they have erred from the faith, and pierced themselves through with many sorrows.

But thou, O man of God, flee these things; and follow after righteousness, godliness, faith, love, patience, meekness.

Fight the good fight of faith, lay hold on eternal life, whereunto thou art also called, and hast professed a good profession before many witnesses.

The teaching form sometimes makes use of dialogue to set forth its lesson. See James 2:14-24, 26. It must be read rather deliberately, almost as though two personalities with differing viewpoints are expressing themselves.

What doth it profit, my brethren, though a man say he hath faith, and have not works? can faith save him?

HOW LOGICAL!

If a brother or sister be naked, and destitute of daily food,

And one of you say unto them, Depart in peace, be ye warmed and filled; notwithstanding ye give them not those things which are needful to the body; what doth it profit?

Even so faith, if it hath not works, is dead, being alone.

Yea, a man may say, Thou hast faith, and I have works: shew me thy faith without thy works, and I will shew thee my faith by my works.

DON'T BE AFRAID TO TELL IT LIKE IT IS

Thou believest that there is one God; thou doest well: the devils also believe, and tremble.

But wilt thou know, O vain man, that faith without works is dead?

Was not Abraham our father justified by works, when he had offered Isaac his son upon the altar?

> Seest thou how faith wrought with his works, and by works was faith made perfect?
>
> And the scripture was fulfilled which saith, Abraham believed God, and it was imputed unto him for righteousness: and he was called the Friend of God.
>
> Ye see then how that by works a man is justified, and not by faith only. . . .
>
> For as the body without the spirit is dead, so faith without works is dead also.

This conversational form is a good medium through which to teach a controversial truth. Don't fail to reflect James's humor in his sanctimonious dismissal of the hungry, naked personality with his "Depart in peace, be ye warmed and filled" when nothing was being done to alleviate his needs. Humor flashes again in the words "You believe that there is one God. You do well. Even the demons believe—and tremble!" (NKJV). The Bible is the most accurate account of human nature ever written. Don't sell its powerful message short by fearing to read it with meaning and significance.

This device of dialogue occurs again in 1 Cor. 15:35-42:

> But some man will say, How are the dead raised up? and with what body do they come?

The answer is,

> Thou fool [and read this gently with a falling inflection; to do otherwise misses the true teaching spirit], that which thou sowest is not quickened, except it die:
>
> And that which thou sowest, thou sowest not that body that shall be, but bare grain, it may chance of wheat, or of some other grain:
>
> But God giveth it a body as it hath pleased him, and to every seed his own body.
>
> All flesh is not the same flesh: but there is one kind of flesh of men, another flesh of beasts, another of fishes, and another of birds.

> There are also celestial bodies, and bodies terrestrial: but the glory of the celestial is one, and the glory of the terrestrial is another.
>
> There is one glory of the sun, and another glory of the moon, and another glory of the stars: for one star differeth from another star in glory.
>
> So also is the resurrection of the dead.

This teaching spirit permeates much of the Bible, for it is indeed a book of instruction.

But a study of the voices of the teachers would be incomplete without giving attention to *Jesus*.

The Master Teacher

We are told, "Never man spake like this man" (John 7:46), and that all in our Lord's hometown synagogue "wondered at the gracious words which proceeded out of his mouth" (Luke 4:22). After hearing His masterful Sermon on the Mount, "The people were astonished at his doctrine: for he taught them as one having authority" (Matt. 7:28-29). He was indeed "a teacher come from God" (John 3:2). If you would have your voice become that of a teacher, study the words of Jesus; read them aloud; partake of His spirit.

Jesus was the living embodiment of the truth He declared. He had a heart of love for those He sought to instruct. The Gospels often record that Christ had compassion on both individuals and large crowds. He had a desire to teach them. Again and again He was called "Teacher." He was master of the art, for He used every method known to educational experts. He was familiar with Scripture and used it to great advantage. He used the facts of everyday life to teach Christianity's most profound truths. He related perfectly to His hearers. We will do well to emulate His methods and His message.

He was always teaching—beside the sea, on the dusty roads of Judea, in the Temple. Perhaps the greatest illustration of Jesus as Teacher is found in the Sermon on the Mount—Matthew 5; 6; and 7. One can delve in anywhere and find perfect teaching material. Try 5:13-16.

> Ye are the salt of the earth: but if the salt have lost his savour, wherewith shall it be salted? it is thenceforth good for nothing, but to be cast out, and to be trodden under foot of men.
>
> Ye are the light of the world. A city that is set on an hill cannot be hid.
>
> Neither do men light a candle, and put it under a bushel, but on a candlestick; and it giveth light unto all that are in the house.
>
> Let your light so shine before men, that they may see your good works, and glorify your Father which is in heaven.

SIMPLE, YET SUBLIME

Try to imagine the Master's voice as He spoke these words—full of command yet of entreaty, strong yet tender, positive yet appealing. The teaching spirit should never become cold and dictatorial. It is always aware that it is dealing with individuals, personalities, not with classes or masses.

Across many years of attempting to assist students to more perfectly and meaningfully read the Word, I have observed that beginners often string words together like beads on a chain, with no pauses to differentiate phrases, and no central words to indicate points of emphasis. A helpful exercise would be to make a copy of the passage you are working on. Then indicate a slash (/) where a pause should occur. Draw a line _____ under a word to indicate it is the central word in that phrase group. Length of inflection can also be shown //, do you see? and direction of inflection, this / or this \. The word receiving the longer inflection will also be the word receiving the greater amount of volume. A good passage to use for such an exercise would be Matt. 5:43-48.

> Ye have heard that it hath been said, Thou shalt love thy neighbour, and hate thine enemy.

> But I say unto you, Love your enemies, bless them that curse you, do good to them that hate you, and pray for them which despitefully use you, and persecute you;
>
> That ye may be the children of your Father which is in heaven: for he maketh his sun to rise on the evil and on the good, and sendeth the rain on the just and on the unjust.
>
> For if ye love them which love you, what reward have ye? do not even the publicans the same?
>
> And if ye salute your brethren only, what do ye more than others? do not even the publicans so?
>
> Be ye therefore perfect, even as your Father which is in heaven is perfect.

EVEN IF IT SEEMS MECHANICAL AT FIRST, KEEP TRYING

Changes of pitch as they occur on the inflected words of each phrase are probably the greatest tool of the teacher in conveying truth. Strive to accentuate the melody in your voice. It should sing a meaningful tune up and down the possibilities of your entire range.

Another great passage is found in Matt. 6:19-33. Punctuation will assist you in determining phrase divisions, though it is not a complete nor an always accurate guide.

> Lay not up for yourselves treasures upon earth, where moth and rust doth corrupt, and where thieves break through and steal:
>
> But lay up for yourselves treasures in heaven, where neither moth nor rust doth corrupt, and where thieves do not break through nor steal.

Contrast is a great device for teaching. Note here that <u>earth,</u> <u>moth and rust,</u> and <u>thieves</u> are set over against <u>heaven,</u> <u>neither,</u> and <u>do not.</u> Ordinarily it is the new idea that receives the emphasis. The idea already before us does not need re-emphasis.

> For where your treasure is, there will your heart be also.

WORK LIKE A PIANIST DOING FIVE-FINGER EXERCISES

> The light of the body is the eye: if therefore thine eye be single, thy whole body shall be full of light.
>
> But if thine eye be evil, thy whole body shall be full of darkness. If therefore the light that is in thee be darkness, how great is that darkness!

The contrast continues—<u>light, eye, single,</u> and <u>light</u> are contrasted with <u>evil, whole body, darkness, how great.</u> These are your emphatic words. They must stand out.

> No man can serve two masters: for either he will hate the one, and love the other; or else he will hold to the one, and despise the other. Ye cannot serve God and mammon.

I am sure you are sensing these contrasts. Nothing can bring them out like the human voice.

There follows one of the most precious and picturesque passages in all the Word of God. It is *argumentum non contestare,* unanswerable logic. God help you to read it so that the attention of your hearers may be arrested in this materialistic age when we are all caught up in the mad scramble for things.

> Therefore I say unto you, Take no thought for your life, what ye shall eat, or what ye shall drink; nor yet for your body, what ye shall put on. Is not the life more than meat, and the body than raiment?

Tenderly, searchingly throw the responsibility for answering this last question back upon your hearers, compelling each to answer the question in the depths of his own soul.

> Behold the fowls of the air: for they sow not, neither do they reap, nor gather into barns; yet your heavenly Father feedeth them. Are ye not much better than they?

Do you see how questions posed form a tremendous asset to the teaching method?

> Which of you by taking thought can add one cubit unto his stature?

> And why take ye thought for raiment? Consider the lilies of the field, how they grow; they toil not, neither do they spin: And yet I say unto you, That even Solomon in all his glory was not arrayed like one of these.
>
> Wherefore, if God so clothe the grass of the field, which to day is, and to morrow is cast into the oven, shall he not much more clothe you, O ye of little faith?

HAVE YOU REACHED THIS SUBLIME LEVEL OF TRUST?

The voice of the teacher is not denunciatory nor condemnatory. It is convincing, illuminating, divinely patient, partaking with the hearers of the great truth being asserted.

> Therefore take no thought, saying, What shall we eat? or, What shall we drink? or, Wherewithal shall we be clothed?

It is not amiss for the voice to give a hint of the agitation and stress that accompany undue anxiety over these material things.

> . . . for your heavenly Father knoweth that ye have need of all these things.

How reassuring! How comforting! The Father is not unaware of the pressures of life. He knows we need food and clothing and shelter. Trust Him. He feeds the birds and clothes the lilies. He is touched by our problems. There is only one requirement that we must meet before His bounty can be released.

> But <u>seek ye first the kingdom of God, and his righteousness</u>; and all these things shall be added unto you.

What things? Food, clothing, housing—all your material needs. But you must first seek His kingdom and His righteousness. Not just to make the equation work, but from your heart and with all your soul, "seek, and ye shall find" (Matt. 7:7). This is unwavering faith put to the test.

This is a lifetime assignment—to make the words of Jesus a living message. But if you will work at it, Bible reading can become an adventure-packed experience.

The Voices of the Poets

Hebrew poetry is lyric. It expresses those emotions stirred by the thought of God. Some poems are addressed *to* God directly in thanksgiving or petition.

> O Lord our Lord, how excellent is thy name in all the earth *(Ps. 8:1)!*
>
> Preserve me, O God: for in thee do I put my trust *(Ps. 16:1).*

Some poems are the communing of the soul *with* God, expressing its faith, its hope, its love, its fears, its aspirations, its joys and triumphs.

> I will love thee, O Lord, my strength.
>
> The Lord is my rock, and my fortress, and my deliverer;
> My God, my strength, in whom I will trust;
> My buckler, and the horn of my salvation,
> And my high tower *(Ps. 18:1-2).*

The lyric is an intensely personal form and must be read with deep realization and the identification of the reader with the words as though he had voiced them in the first place. Emotion will stir the vibrant color of the voice in response to the soul of the reader.

> Unto thee, O Lord, do I lift up my soul.
>
> O my God, I trust in thee:
> Let me not be ashamed,
> Let not mine enemies triumph over me *(Ps. 25:1-2).*
>
> I will bless the Lord at all times:
> His praise shall continually be in my mouth.

My soul shall make her boast in the Lord:
The humble shall hear thereof, and be glad *(Ps. 34:1-2)*.

Hear my cry, O God; attend unto my prayer.

LET YOUR HEART SPEAK

From the end of the earth will I cry unto thee,
When my heart is overwhelmed:
Lead me to the rock that is higher than I *(Ps. 61:1-2)*.

O come, let us sing unto the Lord:
Let us make a joyful noise
To the rock of our salvation.

Let us come before his presence with thanksgiving,
And make a joyful noise unto him with psalms *(Ps. 95:1-2)*.

Some poems celebrate the works of God in *nature*.

The heavens declare the glory of God;
And the firmament sheweth his handywork *(Ps. 19:1)*.

Great is the Lord, and greatly to be praised
In the city of our God, in the mountain of his holiness *(Ps. 48:1)*.

Other poems reflect the perplexing *problems of life* and suggest God as the only reasonable answer. Here the voice of the reader will suggest a change from despair to hope, from perplexity to assurance.

Why art thou cast down, O my soul?
And why art thou disquieted within me?
Hope in God: for I shall yet praise him,
Who is the health of my countenance, and my God *(Ps. 43:5)*.

As the earth revolves around the sun, Hebrew poetry revolves around the revelation of God to the human heart. He is its light and its heat.

In order to interpret the voices of the poets, we must understand the form in which they wrote. The basic structure of biblical poetry is not rhyme or meter. It is parallelism, a balance of clauses or thoughts, relatively equal in length. Only the human voice can completely bring out the beauty of this form. Once felt, it produces a stately rhythm that accentuates rather than detracts from the meaning of the passage. Rhythm is its chief means of expression—the alternation of speech and silence that actually means a skillful use in the variation of volume on important and unimportant words balanced by meaningful pauses. In more recent versions, the poetic structure emerges visually in the printed form.

Various types of parallelism have been analyzed:

Synonymous—where the two lines convey the same meaning

> I will sing of the mercies of the Lord for ever:
> With my mouth will I make known thy faithfulness to all generations *(Ps. 89:1).*

Antithetic—where the second line introduces a contrary thought

> Weeping may endure for a night,
> But joy cometh in the morning *(Ps. 30:5).*

Synthetic—where the thought is expanded, each line building on the first

> Blessed is the man that walketh not in the counsel of the ungodly,
> Nor standeth in the way of sinners,
> Nor sitteth in the seat of the scornful *(Ps. 1:1).*

Awareness of this structural form makes the oral reading of it more significant. The same form applies to verse 3 of Psalm 1.

> And he shall be like a tree planted by the rivers of water,
> That bringeth forth his fruit in his season;
> His leaf also shall not wither;
> And whatsoever he doeth shall prosper.

There is a definite kinship of the poetry of the Psalms with prayer, and many of these expressions of outpoured emotion are actually prayers. This is why they have universal appeal. They speak the language of the individual human heart. Sorrow for sin, repentance, hope, faith, a crying out for help, and assurance are all expressed. The reader must first feel these emotions himself. Then a responsive voice will portray them.

One of the most noble and best-loved psalms is Psalm 27. It is a powerful assertion of faith in God and of total dependence upon Him. It is frequently sung, for it has been set to appropriate and inspiring music, the background memory of which will actually assist the oral reader.

It must not be assumed that, since we have moved on in the progress of this book, the basic elements stressed in the earlier chapters can now be ignored. The pattern of preparation must be followed with each new selection. First, what is the message of this passage? Its title, if you please?

The fundamental idea in this 27th psalm to be lodged in the mind of the hearers is *confidence in our trustworthy God.*

The first declarations are given in full voice with joy and convincing assurance. Find your phrase divisions, locate your central words. Do this orally by trial and error if need be until you are satisfied. The rate is steady, the rhythmic pulsations are strong. The key words stand out: *Lord, light, salvation, strength.*

The recognition of the problems is introduced on a lower pitch with more rapid rate—the *wicked,* the besieging *host,* even *war.* Through it all, our confidence in God is unshaken. He is faithful.

The Psalmist now declares his own fidelity to God: *One thing have I desired of the Lord.* The mood becomes more self-revealing, more intimate. He is safe in God's pavilion. And in joyous praise he gives thanks to God. The voice is radiant with emotion. The reader identifies with the author.

The next verses introduce a form of dialogue. They become more conversational. Changes of pitch will predominate. But they are relieved and elevated by petitions for guidance, for protection, and for sustenance.

The climax of the psalm is an injunction to patience spoken to the hearers and to the author himself as well. But it is spoken with assurance.

"I know!" "I have tried it!" "I recommend God to you!"

Wait on the Lord! He will not fail you! He will never let you down!

READ IT WITH CONFIDENCE

> The Lord is my light and my salvation;
>   whom shall I fear?
> The Lord is the strength of my life;
>   of whom shall I be afraid?
>
> When the wicked, even mine enemies
>   and my foes,
> came upon me to eat up my flesh,
> They stumbled and fell.
>
> Though an host should encamp against me,
>   my heart shall not fear:
> Though war should rise against me,
>   in this will I be confident.
>
> One thing have I desired of the Lord,
>   that will I seek after;
> That I may dwell in the house of the Lord
>   all the days of my life,
> To behold the beauty of the Lord,
>   and to enquire in his temple.
>
> For in the time of trouble
>   he shall hide me in his pavilion:
> In the secret of his tabernacle shall he hide me;
>   he shall set me up upon a rock.
>
> And now shall mine head be lifted up
>   above mine enemies round about me:
> Therefore will I offer in his tabernacle
>   sacrifices of joy;
> I will sing, yea, I will sing praises
>   unto the Lord.
>
> Hear, O Lord, when I cry with my voice:
>   have mercy also upon me, and answer me.

> When thou saidst, Seek ye my face;
>> My heart said unto thee,
>> Thy face, Lord, will I seek.
>
> Hide not thy face far from me;
>> put not thy servant away in anger:
> Thou hast been my help;
>> leave me not, neither forsake me,
>> O God of my salvation.
>
> When my father and my mother forsake me,
>> then the Lord will take me up.
>
> Teach me thy way, O Lord,
>> and lead me in a plain path,
>>> because of mine enemies.
>
> Deliver me not over unto the will of mine enemies:
>> for false witnesses are risen up against me,
>>> and such as breathe out cruelty.
>
> I had fainted, unless I had believed
>> to see the goodness of the Lord
>>> in the land of the living.
>
> Wait on the Lord: be of good courage,
>> and he shall strengthen thine heart:
>>> wait, I say, on the Lord.

We have discussed the poetry of the Bible as it is found in the Psalms. But it occurs in many other places. Wherever emotion causes a personal outburst of feeling, the form becomes lyric. Note Miriam's song in Exod. 15:1 after the successful crossing of the Red Sea:

> I will sing unto the Lord,
> For he hath triumphed gloriously.

Consider David's lament over his slain son Absalom in 2 Sam. 18:33:

> And the king was much moved, and went up to the chamber over the gate, and wept: and as he went, thus he said,
>> O my son Absalom,
>> My son, my son Absalom!

> Would God I had died for thee,
> O Absalom, my son, my son!

Though the son was a traitor to the nation and to the king, the father-heart of David is torn with anguish over his lost son. The voice of the reader can suggest this deep sorrow as he puts himself in the place of David.

Brief lyrical passages are found in the historical books, the Prophets, and even in the Epistles. Examples follow. Read them with a resonant, expressive voice, a respect for their rhythmic movement, and with sufficient melody to give them meaning and save them from monotony on the one hand or sentimentality on the other.

> Lo, the winter is past,
>   The rain is over and gone;
> The flowers appear on the earth;
>   The time of the singing of birds is come,
> And the voice of the turtle is heard in our land *(Song of Sol. 2:11-12)*.

VIVID IMAGERY! VIBRANT EMOTION!

> O Lord, thou art my God;
> I will exalt thee,
> I will praise thy name;
> For thou hast done wonderful things;
> Thy counsels of old are faithfulness and truth. . . .

EMOTIONS RISE, STEP BY STEP LIKE A CLIMB UP A GOLDEN STAIRCASE

> For thou hast been a strength to the poor,
> A strength to the needy in his distress,
> A refuge from the storm,
> A shadow from the heat,
> When the blast of the terrible ones
> Is as a storm against the wall *(Isa. 25:1, 4)*.

> Ye shall go out with joy,
> And be led forth with peace:
> The mountains and the hills
> Shall break forth before you into singing,
> And all the trees of the field
> Shall clap their hands *(Isa. 55:12)*.

> Blessed be the God and Father of our Lord Jesus Christ,
> Which according to his abundant mercy
> Hath begotten us again unto a lively hope
> By the resurrection of Jesus Christ from the dead,
>
> To an inheritance incorruptible, and undefiled,
> And that fadeth not away,
> Reserved in heaven for you,
>
> Who are kept by the power of God
> Through faith unto salvation
> Ready to be revealed in the last time *(1 Pet. 1:3-5).*

Joy, uplift, and spiritual ecstasy produce this outburst of holy delight. To read these glorious, praiseful words in a cold, matter-of-fact tone of voice is to reveal either the speaker's lack of capacity for deep realization or his ignorance as to the power and capability of the human voice. It is not phony exaggeration we are listening for. It is genuine participation of the reader with the mood and experience of the writer. Feeling the emotion that consumed him, the practice of re-creating this response will free the voice to express it. Try it! Alone and aloud. Let the emotion possess you! It may come out first in a cracked voice or even in incapacitating weeping. But learn to conserve your tears until, under the control of a disciplined mind and an utterly sincere spirit, you can plumb the depths of feeling reached in these and many other superb passages from God's Word. They are beautiful melodies. Let them ring in your own soul, and then in your trained and responsive voice.

One can only truly sense the voices of the poets by reading these inspired lyrics aloud. And remember, "Impression precedes and determines expression" (Curry).

The Voices of the Prophets

The calling of the Hebrew prophets was not alone to foretell the future. They were men and women with a message for their own generation. They were to "forth-tell" as well as to "foretell." We should note that they did look down the long corridors of time and prophesy the calamities that were to befall their rebellious and stiff-necked nation—the Babylonian Captivity, the destruction of Jerusalem in A.D. 70, and the scattering of the Jews among all the nations of the earth.

They also foretold the coming of the Messiah:

And there shall come forth a rod out of the stem of Jesse,
And a Branch shall grow out of his roots:

And the spirit of the Lord shall rest upon him,
The spirit of wisdom and understanding,
The spirit of counsel and might,
The spirit of knowledge and of the fear of the Lord;

And shall make him of quick understanding
In the fear of the Lord:
And he shall not judge after the sight of his eyes,
Neither reprove after the hearing of his ears:

But with righteousness shall he judge the poor,
And reprove with equity for the meek of the earth:
And he shall smite the earth with the rod of his mouth,
And with the breath of his lips shall he slay the wicked.

And righteousness shall be the girdle of his loins,
And faithfulness the girdle of his reins. . . .

> . . . For the earth shall be full of the knowledge of the Lord,
> As the waters cover the sea.
>
> And in that day there shall be a root of Jesse,
> Which shall stand for an ensign of the people;
> To it shall the Gentiles seek:
> And his rest shall be glorious *(Isa. 11:1-5, 9-10).*

These prophets also foretold the suffering and death of the Lord as He became the Atonement for our sins.

> He is despised and rejected of men;
> A man of sorrows, and acquainted with grief:
> And we hid as it were our faces from him;
> He was despised, and we esteemed him not.
>
> Surely he hath borne our griefs,
> And carried our sorrows:
> Yet we did esteem him stricken,
> Smitten of God, and afflicted. . . .
>
> He was oppressed, and he was afflicted,
> Yet he opened not his mouth:
> He is brought as a lamb to the slaughter,
> And as a sheep before her shearers is dumb,
> So he openeth not his mouth.
>
> He was taken from prison and from judgment:
> And who shall declare his generation?
> For he was cut off out of the land of the living:
> For the transgression of my people was he stricken.
>
> And he made his grave with the wicked,
> And with the rich in his death;
> Because he had done no violence,
> Neither was any deceit in his mouth *(Isa. 53:3-4, 7-9).*

And John the Revelator, exiled to the island of Patmos for his faith, prophesied:

> . . . I heard the voice of many angels round about the throne and the beasts and the elders: and the number of them was ten thousand times ten thousand, and thousands of thousands;
>
> Saying with a loud voice, Worthy is the Lamb that was slain to receive power, and riches, and wisdom, and strength, and honour, and glory, and blessing *(Rev. 5:11-12).*

The prophets also foretold the second coming of the Lord.

> Who is this that cometh from Edom,
> With dyed garments from Bozrah?
> This that is glorious in his apparel,
> Travelling in the greatness of his strength?
> I that speak in righteousness,
> Mighty to save.
>
> Wherefore art thou red in thine apparel,
> And thy garments like him
> That treadeth in the winefat?
>
> I have trodden the winepress alone;
> And of the people there was none with me:
> For I will tread them in mine anger,
> And trample them in my fury;
> And their blood shall be sprinkled upon my garments,
> And I will stain all my raiment.
>
> For the day of vengeance is in mine heart,
> And the year of my redeemed is come *(Isa. 63:1-4)*.

And the voice of Peter the apostle is added to that of the Old Testament seers.

> Beloved, be not ignorant of this one thing, that one day is with the Lord as a thousand years, and a thousand years as one day.
>
> The Lord is not slack concerning his promise, as some men count slackness; but is longsuffering to us-ward, not willing that any should perish, but that all should come to repentance.
>
> But the day of the Lord will come as a thief in the night; in the which the heavens shall pass away with a great noise, and the elements shall melt with fervent heat, the earth also and the works that are therein shall be burned up.
>
> Seeing then that all these things shall be dissolved, what manner of persons ought ye to be in all holy conversation and godliness,
>
> Looking for and hasting unto the coming of the day of God, wherein the heavens being on fire shall be dissolved, and the elements shall melt with fervent heat?

> Nevertheless we, according to his promise, look for new heavens and a new earth, wherein dwelleth righteousness.
>
> Wherefore, beloved, seeing that ye look for such things, be diligent that ye may be found of him in peace, without spot, and blameless (2 *Pet.* 3:8-14).

The prophets of the Bible were indeed the announcers of things to come. They foretold events scheduled to occur as God's plan for the nations unfolded. But they were especially anointed by God to speak against the wickedness of their own day, the idolatry, the corruption, the greed, and the blindness in both the political and the religious life of their time.

These were fearless in their denunciations, even suffering martyrdom for their courageous and unpopular declarations. They were powerful in their passion for truth. And they were unshakable in their faith in the ultimate triumph of the sovereignty of God. Through all their dark predictions runs the bright promise that finally "the earth shall be filled with the knowledge of the glory of the Lord, as the waters cover the sea" (Hab. 2:14; see Isa. 11:9). They were seers (see-ers). They took a long look upon the entire plan of God for the human race. Yet they were the conscience of their day, probing, warning, rebuking the individual for indifference and failure. They were the statesmen of their nation, spokesmen for God, declaring His will for His chosen people.

They dealt always in abiding and universal truth, so that their messages are as relevant for our day as for the times in which they were spoken.

Note the "woes" in Isaiah 5: Woe unto the unscrupulous and greedy land grabbers (v. 8); woe unto the drunkards and the mad and irreverent pleasure seekers (vv. 11-12); woe unto the scoffers who blaspheme the name and power of God (vv. 18-19); woe unto those leaders who willfully deceive the people who look to them for guidance (v. 20); woe unto the unprincipled bigots (v. 21); woe unto the accepters of bribes who for money wrest justice and oppress the righteous (v. 23). Hear the *judgments* of God upon all such.

> Therefore as the fire devoureth the stubble,
> And the flame consumeth the chaff,
> So their root shall be as rottenness,
> And their blossom shall go up as dust:
> Because they have cast away the law of the Lord of hosts,
> And despised the word of the Holy One of Israel (5:24).

I challenge anyone who grasps the meaning of these passages to read them in a soft, weak, apologetic tone of voice. Practice upon the words of the prophets will give to one's preaching and teaching a note of authority and conviction, an unmistakable "thus saith the Lord."

But note also that the prophets were tender, compassionate men. They were firm, unequivocal in their positions. Yet they were persuasive. There runs the pleading note through all their pronouncements.

> Wash you, make you clean;
> Put away the evil of your doings from before mine eyes;
> Cease to do evil;
>
> Learn to do well;
> Seek judgment, relieve the oppressed,
> Judge the fatherless, plead for the widow.
> Come now, and let us reason together,
> Saith the Lord:
> Though your sins be as scarlet,
> They shall be as white as snow;
> Though they be red like crimson,
> They shall be as wool (Isa. 1:16-18).

HOW RELEVANT FOR OUR DAY!

The prophets were personally involved. They were the mouthpiece of God, but the outcome mattered to them. If we are to properly interpret them, it must matter to *us*. As their interpreters, we cannot become merely condemnatory and vitriolic. Love must temper indignation; willingness to forgive must ever be the condition of judgment. There is always a note of hope even in the darkest day. This must ring out.

> He will swallow up death in victory;
> And the Lord God will wipe away tears
> From off all faces;
> And the rebuke of his people shall he take away
> From off all the earth:
> For the Lord hath spoken it.
>
> And it shall be said in that day,
> Lo, this is our God;
> We have waited for him, and he will save us:
> This is the Lord;
> We have waited for him,
> We will be glad and rejoice in his salvation *(Isa. 25:8-9).*

These favorite passages come from the lips of the mighty prophet Isaiah:

> Thou wilt keep him in perfect peace,
> Whose mind is stayed on thee:
> Because he trusteth in thee.
>
> Trust ye in the Lord for ever:
> For in the Lord Jehovah is everlasting strength *(Isa. 26:3-4).*
>
> I will bring the blind by a way that they knew not;
> I will lead them in paths that they have not known:
> I will make darkness light before them,
> And crooked things straight.
> These things will I do unto them,
> And not forsake them *(Isa. 42:16).*

WHAT CONFIDENCE THIS INSPIRES!

There is another characteristic of the voice of the prophet. He speaks always for a verdict. He demands a decision. This fact differentiates this form from all others. The storyteller relates, the historian recounts, the teacher instructs, the poet sings. Their purpose is veiled. They leave the results with the hearer.

But the prophet draws the issue. He presents the alternatives. The hearer is faced with accepting or rejecting. The prophet is decisive. Repeat the words of Joshua.

Choose you this day whom ye will serve; whether the gods which your fathers served that were on the other side of the flood, or the gods of the Amorites, in whose land ye dwell: but as for me and my house, we will serve the Lord.

And the people answered and said, God forbid that we should forsake the Lord, to serve other gods; . . .

. . . The Lord our God will we serve, and his voice will we obey *(Josh. 24:15-16, 24).*

Elijah also, as he set the stage on Mount Carmel for the contest between the prophets of Baal and himself, cried out to the children of Israel:

How long halt ye between two opinions? if the Lord be God, follow him: but if Baal, then follow him *(1 Kings 18:21).*

The Master, too, calls for a decision. The voice must clearly indicate the imperatives.

Ask, and it shall be given you;
  Seek, and ye shall find;
    Knock, and it shall be opened unto you.

For every one that asketh receiveth;
  And he that seeketh findeth;
    And to him that knocketh it shall be opened.

CALL FOR A VERDICT! If a son shall ask bread of any of you that is a father, will he give him a stone? or if he ask a fish, will he for a fish give him a serpent?

Or if he shall ask an egg, will he offer him a scorpion?

If ye then, being evil, know how to give good gifts unto your children: how much more shall your heavenly Father give the Holy Spirit to them that ask him? *(Luke 11:9-13).*

The voice of the prophet has distinct qualities that differentiate it from that used in all other literary forms. It has a measurable degree of volume. This must have variation, of course, to prevent monotony. But it must have strength and intensity. Practice upon such passages as the following will develop this quality. It is not mere loudness. It is the voice of authority.

> Cry aloud, spare not, lift up thy voice like a trumpet, and shew my people their transgression, and the house of Jacob their sins *(Isa. 58:1).*
>
> Arise, shine; for thy light is come, and the glory of the Lord is risen upon thee.
>
> For, behold, the darkness shall cover the earth, and gross darkness the people: but the Lord shall arise upon thee, and his glory shall be seen upon thee.
>
> And the Gentiles shall come to thy light, and kings to the brightness of thy rising *(Isa. 60:1-3).*

Wide changes in pitch will reveal contrasts such as those from light to darkness.

> I have set watchmen upon thy walls, O Jerusalem, which shall never hold their peace day nor night: ye that make mention of the Lord, keep not silence,
>
> And give him no rest, till he establish, and till he make Jerusalem a praise in the earth *(Isa. 62:6-7).*

The voice of the prophet does not become harsh or vindictive. A moving persuasion is always present. He is the intermediary between a just and righteous God and weak, straying, sinful humanity. He must interpret the compassion of the Father as well as His holiness.

> For thus saith the high and lofty One that inhabiteth eternity, whose name is Holy; I dwell in the high and holy place, with him also that is of a contrite and humble spirit, to revive the spirit of the humble, and to revive the heart of the contrite ones *(Isa. 57:15).*
>
> I know the thoughts that I think toward you, saith the Lord, thoughts of peace, and not of evil, to give you an expected end [or as the Rotherham Version has it: I know the plans that I am planning for you, plans of welfare and not of calamity, to give you a future and a hope].
>
> Then shall ye call upon me, and ye shall go and pray unto me, and I will hearken unto you.

And ye shall seek me, and find me, when ye shall search for me with all your heart *(Jer. 29:11-13)*.

Great confidence, great assurance must be heard in the voice of the prophet. And there is no way this can be conveyed to the hearer except that it be the inmost possession of the reader. His confidence in the Word of God must be absolute. His conviction that he speaks the truth must be firm and unshaken. His experience must have convinced him that not one promise shall fail of complete fulfillment. Familiarity with the passage is not enough. It must have become a definite persuasion on the part of the speaker. Otherwise, his words are hollow, and his posture as the interpreter of the prophets is a mockery. Head and heart are both involved. Mind and spirit must unite. Nothing will so strengthen your delivery, preacher or reader, as will the oral rendering of the words of the prophets as they are revealed to you by the Spirit of God.

IS HIS WORD YOUR POSSESSION?

The Voices of Sublime Truth

We have discussed the voices of the Bible—the voices of the storyteller, the teacher, the poet, the prophet. They all proclaim divine truth. Together their declarations constitute the Divine Word. They all are a part of the inspiration that has come to men from the Holy Spirit of God and which is recorded in the Book we call the Bible.

But there is another Voice resounding throughout all of Scripture. In this great Symphony of Truth, its tones are purer and sweeter, its quality is finer and more lofty. The exaltation of its sublime utterances throbs through and mingles with all the other voices. This Voice sounds a message of eternal and universal truth, a note so elevated and comprehensive that it belongs to all men of every generation and of every race. It awakens affirmation in every soul that is attuned to hear. It belongs to the whole human family, and it identifies with it.

THE GREATEST VOICE OF ALL

It is epic in scope and in grandeur. It is an essential element of the divine revelation. It explains in part why the Bible has universal appeal.

These majestic passages can only be truly expressed by the human voice. On the printed page they do not have prominence. Their worth can be demonstrated only as they are given utterance. Then they shine like precious stones in a golden setting. They are indeed gems—gems of eternal truth. They are clothed in words of sublimest beauty and yet in the simplest of language.

The woman taken in the act of adultery and dragged by the scribes and Pharisees before Jesus for His condemnation heard such epic words (John 8:1-11). After the Master had written in the sand (and how we wish we knew what He wrote; keep the mystery in it as you read), He said, "He that is without sin among you, let him first cast a stone at her." One by one, the religious defenders of the law withdrew, convicted by their own conscience.

Left then with no one but the Master to accuse her, she heard those matchless words, "Neither do I condemn thee: go, and sin no more." Words spoken first to her, but after her to all, that all may always know He has "power on earth to forgive sins" (Mark 2:10 et al.). Epic words!

These sublime utterances are not found in any given chapters or verses of the Bible. They are not only found in the pronouncements of God the Father, nor of Jesus Christ His Son. They do not belong exclusively to any of the Bible authors—storyteller, teacher, poet, or prophet. They run like a golden thread throughout the whole revelation. They shine out in splendor from every literary form. Where properly expressed, they communicate their lofty message to the hearers, though these hearers might not be able to analyze their response.

Five areas or classifications into which these noble utterances may be arranged now follow.

The Great Affirmations

First are the great affirmations of the Word of God. One is overwhelmed by the number and by the power of these declarations, though they appear in individual settings and often are spoken to specific individuals; yet amazingly, their truth is so lofty and their appeal so universal that they assume for us all a very real and personal application.

These strong declarations from God's Word must be given with deep conviction. This will mean a consistent degree of volume that is not mere loudness. There is a difference!

Volume implies good breath control to produce a confident tone of voice. To increase volume does not mean the elimination of the other expressive modulations of the voice. The central words receiving the greater touch or ictus will also receive the longer inflection. Lower changes of pitch will convey subordinate ideas. There will be meaningful pauses. Changes of rate will indicate mood changes. Technique must be present. But technique is sublimated to lofty thought and noble emotion. Then technique becomes your tool, not your aim.

The note to be struck is one of personal testimony, personal assurance. This gives a ring of certainty to the voice.

The Psalms abound in epic lines. No book in the Bible identifies more closely with human experience. Here are some examples:

> Trust in the Lord, and do good; so shalt thou dwell in the land, and verily thou shalt be fed.
>
> Delight thyself also in the Lord; and he shall give thee the desires of thine heart.
>
> Commit thy way unto the Lord; trust also in him; and he shall bring it to pass.
>
> And he shall bring forth thy righteousness as the light, and thy judgment as the noonday.
>
> Rest in the Lord . . . *(Ps. 37:3-7).*
>
> God is our refuge and strength, a very present help in trouble *(Ps. 46:1).*
>
> I will instruct thee and teach thee in the way which thou shalt go: I will guide thee with mine eye *(Ps. 32:8).*
>
> The Lord God is a sun and shield: the Lord will give grace and glory: no good thing will he withhold from them that walk uprightly *(Ps. 84:11).*
>
> I will lift up mine eyes unto the hills, from whence cometh my help.

> My help cometh from the Lord, which made heaven and earth (Ps. 121:1-2).
>
> The Lord is nigh unto all them that call upon him, to all that call upon him in truth (Ps. 145:18).

The Book of Isaiah, too, abounds in strong declarations of a faith that triumphs over even adverse conditions and extreme difficulties.

> They that wait upon the Lord shall renew their strength; they shall mount up with wings as eagles; they shall run, and not be weary; and they shall walk, and not faint (Isa. 40:31).
>
> **CAN YOU SENSE THE SUBLIMITY OF THESE LINES?**
>
> For the Lord God will help me; therefore shall I not be confounded: therefore have I set my face like a flint, and I know that I shall not be ashamed (Isa. 50:7).
>
> O thou afflicted, tossed with tempest, and not comforted, behold, I will lay thy stones with fair colours, and lay thy foundations with sapphires. . . .
>
> And all thy children shall be taught of the Lord; and great shall be the peace of thy children (Isa. 54:11, 13).
>
> For thus saith the high and lofty One that inhabiteth eternity, whose name is Holy; I dwell in the high and holy place, with him also that is of a contrite and humble spirit, to revive the spirit of the humble, and to revive the heart of the contrite ones (Isa. 57:15).

Jeremiah, the weeping prophet, speaks out with some of the mightiest affirmations to be found in the entire Bible.

> Call unto me, and I will answer thee, and shew thee great and mighty things, which thou knowest not (Jer. 33:3).

The following powerful assurance has brought comfort to thousands.

> It is of the Lord's mercies that we are not consumed, because his compassions fail not.
>
> They are new every morning: great is thy faithfulness (Lam. 3:22-23).

The prophets, the seers, rose to epic declarations again and again.

> I will pour out my spirit upon all flesh; and your sons and your daughters shall prophesy, your old men shall dream dreams, your young men shall see visions:
>
> And also upon the servants and upon the handmaids in those days will I pour out my spirit (Joel 2:28-29).

DOES YOUR VOICE EXPRESS THE LOFTINESS OF THESE THOUGHTS?

> He hath shewed thee, O man, what is good; and what doth the Lord require of thee, but to do justly, and to love mercy, and to walk humbly with thy God? (Mic. 6:8).

These words that follow are those of John the Baptist, who prepared the way for the Messiah.

> I indeed baptize you with water unto repentance: but he that cometh after me is mightier than I, whose shoes I am not worthy to bear: he shall baptize you with the Holy Ghost, and with fire:
>
> Whose fan is in his hand, and he will throughly purge his floor, and gather his wheat into the garner; but he will burn up the chaff with unquenchable fire (Matt. 3:11-12).

Epic lines appear in many narratives recorded in both the Old and New Testaments.

In the story of Jacob, wrestling with the angel at the brook Peniel as recorded in Gen. 32:24-30, are these words realized personally by many who have experienced a similar struggle:

Jacob: I will not let thee go, except thou bless me.

The Wrestler: As a prince hast thou power with God and with men, and hast prevailed.

The Narrator: And he blessed him there.

Sublime words of universal truth, realized by many who have been vindicated after suffering wrongfully, occur in the story of Joseph as he revealed his identity to his stricken brothers.

> Ye thought evil against me; but God meant it unto good *(Gen. 50:20).*

Moses and the children of Israel at the Red Sea hear these reassuring words from God. They have spoken also to unnumbered believers.

> Fear ye not, stand still, and see the salvation of the Lord . . . The Lord shall fight for you, and ye shall hold your peace *(Exod. 14:13-14).*

Moses' word to Joshua has been claimed by many undertaking to build the kingdom of God upon earth.

> Be strong and of a good courage . . . for the Lord thy God, he it is that doth go with thee; he will not fail thee, nor forsake thee. . . . fear not, neither be dismayed *(Deut. 31:6, 8).*

Beautiful lines from the story of Ruth hold for me personally an epic significance.

I cared for my blind and bedfast father during the last years of his life. It was a confining task. But it was a labor of love, and never for one moment did I wish it otherwise. But occasionally the walls of the home did close in around me. My husband was gone most of the time, fulfilling his duties to the general church. My family was supportive, and without this I could not have made it. But friends wearied of coming to brighten my days or became accustomed to my circumstances. I knew great loneliness.

One morning I wakened with an unusual sense of the presence of the Lord in the room. Indeed, so real was it that I felt had I wakened a moment earlier, I might actually have seen Him.

And these words were in my mind: "The Lord recompense thy work, and a full reward be given thee of the Lord God of Israel, under whose wings thou art come to trust" (Ruth 2:12).

I had learned the passage at my mother's behest many years before. I was not at the moment even able to put it in its setting. But it was quickened to me in a most personal way. "The Lord recompense THY work, and a full reward be given THEE." Reward *always* follows total commitment. It was and is universally true, for Ruth and for me and for us all!

Hear these majestic affirmations from the lips of Job when he was sorely afflicted.

> I know that my redeemer liveth, and that he shall stand at the latter day upon the earth:
>
> And after my skin has been destroyed (NIV), yet in my flesh shall I see God:
>
> Whom I shall see for myself, and mine eyes shall behold, and not another *(Job 19:25-27).*

STAND ON TIPTOE TO READ IT WELL!

> He knoweth the way that I take: when he hath tried me, I shall come forth as gold *(Job 23:10).*

This is eternal truth! Job had superlative faith—echoed, too, from the heart of everyone who has had a personal confrontation with the resurrected Christ. Job's faith reached down the dimly lighted corridors of time before His advent! How much more quickly should we appropriate such faith as we look back to the fact accomplished. With what sublime confidence these words are uttered. They must be read with the assurance that is inherent in them.

God's word to Solomon in 2 Chron. 7:14 is as applicable to our day as to his.

> If my people, which are called by my name, shall humble themselves, and pray, and seek my face, and turn from their wicked ways; then will I hear from heaven, and will forgive their sin, and will heal their land.

The New Testament also yields its rich treasures of epic lines.

> With men this is impossible; but with God all things are possible *(Matt. 19:26).*

The Son of man came not to be ministered unto, but to minister, and to give his life a ransom for many *(Mark 10:45)*.

There is no man that hath left house, or parents, or brethren, or wife, or children, for the kingdom of God's sake,

Who shall not receive manifold more in this present time, and in the world to come life everlasting *(Luke 18:29-30)*.

The Word was made flesh, and dwelt among us, (and we beheld his glory, the glory as of the only begotten of the Father,) full of grace and truth *(John 1:14)*.

God so loved the world, that he gave his only begotten Son, that whosoever believeth in him should not perish, but have everlasting life *(John 3:16)*.

Ye shall know the truth, and the truth shall make you free *(John 8:32)*.

MAKE IT PERSONAL, THEN MAKE IT BIG!

Whatsoever ye shall ask in my name, that will I do, that the Father may be glorified in the Son *(John 14:13)*.

My God shall supply all your need according to his riches in glory by Christ Jesus *(Phil. 4:19)*.

Psalm 24 is one of the most sublime passages in all the Word of God. These words were probably sung antiphonally by great choirs massed upon the hills surrounding the Temple area. The voices were accompanied by stringed instruments and organs; the flute, the cornet, and the trumpet; loud cymbals and high-sounding cymbals.

The human voice can suggest this alternating grandeur of sound when the imagination of the reader is fired by the glory of the scene.

All Voices in Unison
> The earth is the Lord's, and the fulness thereof;
> The world, and they that dwell therein.
> For he hath founded it upon the seas,
> And established it upon the floods.

Choir I
> Who shall ascend into the hill of the Lord?
> Or who shall stand in his holy place?

Solo Voice
> He that hath clean hands, and a pure heart;
> Who hath not lifted up his soul unto vanity,
> Nor sworn deceitfully.

Choir II
> He shall receive the blessing from the Lord,
> And righteousness from the God of his salvation.

Both Choirs
> This is the generation of them that seek him,
> That seek thy face, O Jacob.

Choir I
> Lift up your heads, O ye gates;
> And be ye lift up, ye everlasting doors;
> And the King of glory shall come in.

Choir II
> Who is this King of glory?

Choir I
> The Lord strong and mighty,
> The Lord mighty in battle.

Choir II
> Lift up your heads, O ye gates;
> Even lift them up, ye everlasting doors;
> And the King of glory shall come in.

Choir I
> Who is this King of glory?

Unison
> The Lord of hosts, he is the King of glory.

The musical directions are, of course, supplied by my own imagination. But try reading the psalm using them. It will make your reading come alive. By the way, the word *Selah* is *not* to be read orally. It was probably a direction given to the musicians.

The universal invitation recorded in Isaiah 55 likewise is almost pure epic. The majesty of its language and the universality of its appeal command our very best in vocal expression.

Ho, every one that thirsteth, come ye to the waters,
And he that hath no money; come ye, buy, and eat;
Yea, come, buy wine and milk
Without money and without price.

Wherefore do ye spend money
For that which is not bread?   **GLORIOUS**
And your labour   **INVITATION**
For that which satisfieth not?

Hearken diligently unto me,
And eat ye that which is good,
And let your soul delight itself in fatness.

Incline your ear, and come unto me:
Hear, and your soul shall live;
And I will make an everlasting covenant with you,
Even the sure mercies of David.

Seek ye the Lord while he may be found,
Call ye upon him while he is near:

Let the wicked forsake his way,
And the unrighteous man his thoughts:
And let him return unto the Lord,
And he will have mercy upon him;
And to our God,
For he will abundantly pardon.

For my thoughts are not your thoughts,
Neither are your ways my ways, saith the Lord.

For as the heavens are higher than the earth,
So are my ways higher than your ways,
And my thoughts than your thoughts.

For as the rain cometh down, and the snow from heaven,
And returneth not thither, but watereth the earth,
And maketh it bring forth and bud,
That it may give seed to the sower, and bread to the eater:

So shall my word be that goeth forth out of my mouth:
It shall not return unto me void,
But it shall accomplish that which I please,
And it shall prosper in the thing whereto I sent it.

For ye shall go out with joy,
And be led forth with peace:

> The mountains and the hills shall break forth before you into singing,
> And all the trees of the field shall clap their hands.
>
> Instead of the thorn
> Shall come up the fir tree,
> And instead of the brier
> Shall come up the myrtle tree:
> And it shall be to the Lord for a name,
> For an everlasting sign that shall not be cut off.

The writers of the Epistles of the New Testament rise to unbelievable heights of eloquence and power as they declare their faith. Hear Paul in Rom. 8:35, 37-39.

> Who shall separate us from the love of Christ? shall tribulation, or distress, or persecution, or famine, or nakedness, or peril, or sword? . . .
>
> Nay, in all these things we are more than conquerors through him that loved us.
>
> For I am persuaded, that neither death, nor life, nor angels, nor principalities, nor powers, nor things present, nor things to come,
>
> Nor height, nor depth, nor any other creature, shall be able to separate us from the love of God, which is in Christ Jesus our Lord.

MAKE THIS YOUR OWN AFFIRMATION

Paul masses together all the things imaginable that could defeat us and then declares that even so, suffering all these setbacks, we are still victors with a margin—more than conquerors. The rough road we may even now be walking turns smooth when we see Christ's footprints there. We accept whatever may be our lot, knowing it is for our good and His glory. Nothing can alienate us from Him who has redeemed us with His own precious blood.

Another one of Paul's great affirmations is found in 1 Cor. 15:51-57.

> Behold, I shew you a mystery; We shall not all sleep, but we shall all be changed,

> In a moment, in the twinkling of an eye, at the last trump: for the trumpet shall sound, and the dead shall be raised incorruptible, and we shall be changed.
>
> For this corruptible must put on incorruption, and this mortal must put on immortality.
>
> So when this corruptible shall have put on incorruption, and this mortal shall have put on immortality, then shall be brought to pass the saying that is written, Death is swallowed up in victory.
>
> O death, where is thy sting? O grave, where is thy victory?
>
> The sting of death is sin; and the strength of sin is the law.
>
> But thanks be to God, which giveth us the victory through our Lord Jesus Christ.

Supreme triumph! Ineffable glory!

The writer to the Hebrews seems in the following passages to have looked even beyond the veil. There in the heavenly Jerusalem, God is seated upon His throne, with Jesus, the Mediator of the new covenant, by His side. The choirs of the redeemed are assembled with an innumerable company of angels. The majestic picture is an invitation to pure and holy living as a prerequisite for entry into this place where holiness reigns supreme.

> Ye are come unto mount Sion, and unto the city of the living God, the heavenly Jerusalem, and to an innumerable company of angels,
>
> To the general assembly and church of the firstborn, which are written in heaven, and to God the Judge of all, and to the spirits of just men made perfect,
>
> And to Jesus the mediator of the new covenant, and to the blood of sprinkling, that speaketh better things than that of Abel. . . .
>
> Wherefore we receiving a kingdom which cannot be moved, let us have grace, whereby we may serve God acceptably with reverence and godly fear *(Heb. 12:22-24, 28).*

The Emotions of Jesus

Another fascinating study of the sublime passages of God's Word may center around the emotions experienced and displayed by Christ the Lord while He was upon earth.

Perhaps an effort to portray His deep feelings through oral reading of the following expressions will convince us that emotion does have a noble and purging effect upon our own religious life. Therefore, if we were to exclude all emotion from our spiritual life, we would destroy it.

What *Compassion* shines through these words:

> Come unto me, all ye that labour and are heavy laden, and I will give you rest.
>
> Take my yoke upon you, and learn of me; for I am meek and lowly in heart: and ye shall find rest unto your souls.
>
> For my yoke is easy, and my burden is light *(Matt. 11:28-30).*

What *Reassurance* in:

> Be of good cheer; it is I; be not afraid *(Matt. 14:27).*

Hear the *Challenge* in this:

> If ye have faith as a grain of mustard seed, ye shall say unto this mountain, Remove hence to yonder place; and it shall remove; and nothing shall be impossible unto you *(Matt. 17:20).*

To those who bought and sold in the Temple, hear the *Rebuke:*

> My house shall be called the house of prayer; but ye have made it a den of thieves *(Matt. 21:13).*

Infinite *Regret* here:

> O Jerusalem, Jerusalem, thou that killest the prophets, and stonest them which are sent unto thee, how often would I have gathered thy children together, even as a hen gathereth her chickens under her wings, and ye would not! *(Matt. 23:37).*

Loneliness and *Anguish:*

> My soul is exceeding sorrowful, even unto death: tarry ye here, and watch with me *(Matt. 26:38).*

Judgment here:

Woe unto you, scribes and Pharisees, hypocrites! for ye pay tithe of mint and anise and cummin, and have omitted the weightier matters of the law, judgment, mercy, and faith: these ought ye to have done, and not to leave the other undone *(Matt. 23:23)*.

Reward in these words:

Come, ye blessed of my Father, inherit the kingdom prepared for you from the foundation of the world:

For I was an hungred, and ye gave me meat: I was thirsty, and ye gave me drink: I was a stranger, and ye took me in:

Naked, and ye clothed me: I was sick, and ye visited me: I was in prison, and ye came unto me *(Matt. 25:34-36)*.

Authority—Sense of Mission:

The Spirit of the Lord is upon me, because he hath anointed me to preach the gospel to the poor; he hath sent me to heal the brokenhearted, to preach deliverance to the captives, and recovering of sight to the blind, to set at liberty them that are bruised,

DOES YOUR VOICE REVEAL THESE SHADES OF EMOTION?

To preach the acceptable year of the Lord *(Luke 4:18-19)*.

Divine Power:

Daughter, be of good comfort: thy faith hath made thee whole; go in peace *(Luke 8:48)*.

Hope and *Sadness:*

The Lord said, Simon, Simon, behold, Satan hath desired to have you, that he may sift you as wheat:

But I have prayed for thee, that thy faith fail not: and when thou art converted, strengthen thy brethren.

And he said unto him, Lord, I am ready to go with thee, both into prison, and to death.

And he said, I tell thee, Peter, the cock shall not crow this day, before that thou shalt thrice deny that thou knowest me *(Luke 22:31-34)*.

Peace:

Peace I leave with you, my peace I give unto you: not as the world giveth, give I unto you. Let not your heart be troubled, neither let it be afraid *(John 14:27).*

Fulfillment:

I have glorified thee on the earth: I have finished the work which thou gavest me to do *(John 17:4).*

Divine *Compulsion:*

I must work the works of him that sent me, while it is day: the night cometh, when no man can work *(John 9:4).*

Perfect *Confidence:*

I am the way, the truth, and the life: no man cometh unto the Father, but by me *(John 14:6).*

FEEL IT AND YOU WILL HEAR IT

Love's Penetrating Test:

So when they had dined, Jesus saith to Simon Peter, Simon, son of Jonas, lovest thou me more than these? He saith unto him, Yea, Lord; thou knowest that I love thee. He saith unto him, Feed my lambs.

He saith unto him again the second time, Simon, son of Jonas, lovest thou me? He saith unto him, Yea, Lord; thou knowest that I love thee. He saith unto him, Feed my sheep.

He saith unto him the third time, Simon, son of Jonas, lovest thou me? Peter was grieved because he said unto him the third time, Lovest thou me? And he said unto him, Lord, thou knowest all things; thou knowest that I love thee. Jesus saith unto him, Feed my sheep *(John 21:15-17).*

The portrayal of the various emotional nuances of which the human voice is capable requires much study and practice. But it is a rewarding task. When you hear yourself saying what you feel, it is an exhilarating experience. Emotion is revealed through the color or quality of the voice. As the body of a stringed musical instrument resonates the sound produced by the bow vibrating the strings, so the delicate human musculature of the entire body responding to an emotion gives timbre or appropriate color to the voice. The body is a whole, the voice a part.

First, then, if we would interpret the gamut of emotions found in Holy Scripture, we must cultivate a responsive body. The face, the eyes will say what we are feeling, and so will the torso, the hands; even the large musculature of the entire trunk will be in harmonious response.

A student mostly hidden behind a massive podium was attempting to read,

> Come unto me, all ye that labour and are heavy laden, and I will give you rest.
>
> Take my yoke upon you—

I stopped him. "You have your left foot draped over your right in a position of total relaxation," I told him. "It is affecting your whole emotional response to those matchless words."

"How did you know?" he muttered, correcting his posture.

"I could hear it!" was my answer.

Emotion is color. Think of a rainbow with its soft green and blue, its delicate mauve, its strong red and orange, its lovely gold. All shades are blended into a perfect harmony. So some emotions are sharp and shocking; some are tender and moving. The voice will respond if you will train it to respond. The primary response is not action, not movement. It is the much more subtle but still apparent reaction of the entire musculature of the body.

A woman stone deaf heard a passage read interpretatively with genuine feeling. Afterward she told the reader, "I followed you all the way!"

The Great Prayers

Prayer is the loftiest expression known to man. Yet it presupposes the deepest humility—the finite addressing the infinite. We should never have the courage to attempt it except that we have been bidden to come. We are assured that God's ear is quick to hear our faintest cry. He has invited us to pray and has promised to hear and answer us.

Prayer at its best is praise, worship, and adoration. It is communion with God; it is thanksgiving; and it is petition. It implies the deepest supplication, a cry from the heart, not merely the lips. It is intercession, when we assume the burdens of others and pray for these burdens as though they were our own. Prayer is confession, and let none presume that they have nothing to confess. Prayer embodies entreaty, the full heart yearning for God, to know His approval, to determine His will.

It is an interesting phenomenon that many Christians especially in public prayer assume an unnatural voice. Some magnify the volume as though God were dead or at least deaf. Often this increased volume will be accompanied by an elimination of pitch or a substitution of a meaningless pattern of pitches so the result is a loud, monotonous sound. It is impossible for this sound to be resonated effectively.

In contrast, others, apparently awed by the thought that mere man can address the Almighty God, reduce volume and eliminate the other expressive actions of the voice until they are scarcely audible. These bad habits can be transferred to the reading of the great prayers of the Bible. Let us avoid them.

Now probably in interpreting scriptural prayers, the voice will assume a lower range. This denotes reverence and humility. It is not, however, a mechanical decision to lower the pitch. It follows a realization of the nature and dignity of true prayer.

Pauses, as well, will be longer, but the silences will be filled with intense realization. A genuine pause is a looking back on what has just been said or a preparation for what is about to be said; maybe both.

Again, in reading the Bible's great prayers, there will be an intensity of feeling revealed in the strong, rhythmic rate of utterance. Take them clause by clause, idea by idea, and attempt to reproduce their depth of meaning.

A study of some of the great prayers of the Bible and the effort to interpret them orally should have a beneficial effect upon our own prayer life. We know so much *about* prayer; we like to hear people talk about prayer. But many of us are powerless in prayer because we spend so little time in the *practice* of prayer. This tremendous asset is ours for the promotion of Christ's kingdom upon earth. Too often we fail to avail ourselves of its power.

Jesus himself is our Example in this. He spent whole nights in prayer. He withdrew into a desert place or a mountaintop alone, and there He met the Father in intimate communion. With the disciples we would say, "Lord, teach *us* to pray" (Luke 11:1).

The Lord's Prayer

Our rendering of the Lord's Prayer, or better the Apostles' Prayer, as found in Matt. 6:9-13, will be a helpful exercise. One must deliberately break away from the mechanical, stereotyped manner in which it is usually given by a congregation with its rapid rate and mumbling diction.

It is a model of simplicity and sincerity. Its opening address suggests close fellowship—<u>Our Father</u>—but it also suggests the deepest reverence—<u>hallowed be thy name. Thy kingdom come</u>—in conquering the world of men. <u>Thy will be done</u>—in my own heart and in every heart. There is no more sublime petition of which man is capable than this—<u>Thy will be done.</u> Read it with total submission.

These first three petitions are for Kingdom interests. The next three are for personal needs: For the supply of physical requirements—<u>Give us our daily bread.</u> For a right relationship with our fellowmen, all in the clear, no grudges, no hidden resentments, no harbored ill will—<u>Forgive us our debts, as we forgive our debtors.</u> Forgive us as we forgive! This is a startling addition to the cry for God's forgiveness. Only as we forgive, in proportion as we forgive, can we be forgiven. And finally a prayer for perfect relationship with God, no condemnation, no taint of sin—<u>Lead us not into temptation, but deliver us from evil.</u>

The conclusion is a fitting acknowledgment of the power and majesty of God. <u>Thine is the kingdom, and the power, and the glory.</u>

REVERENTLY ATTEMPT THESE GREAT PRAYERS

The perfect prayer! All inclusive!

Our Father which art in heaven,
> Hallowed be thy name.
> Thy kingdom come.
> Thy will be done
>> in earth, as it is in heaven.
> Give us this day our daily bread.
> And forgive us our debts,
>> as we forgive our debtors.
> And lead us not into temptation,
>> but deliver us from evil:
For thine is the kingdom,
> and the power,
>> and the glory, for ever. Amen.

Moses' Prayer for Israel

One of the greatest intercessory prayers ever breathed out came from the lips of Moses. It is recorded in Exod. 32:30-32.

You remember the setting. While Moses tarried on Mount Sinai, receiving the Ten Commandments from God, the people persuaded Aaron to make them a golden calf before which they were worshiping when he returned.

And Moses' anger was kindled against the people, and God's anger was kindled, and He was ready to destroy them.

"And it came to pass on the morrow, that Moses said unto the people, <u>Ye have sinned a great sin: and now I will go up unto the Lord; peradventure I shall make an atonement for your sin.</u>

"And Moses returned unto the Lord, and said, <u>Oh, this people have sinned a great sin, and have made them gods of gold.</u>

"<u>Yet now, if thou wilt forgive their sin—; and if not, blot me, I pray thee, out of thy book which thou hast written.</u>"

Perhaps nowhere except in Gethsemane do we hear such a cry. Does the clause "If thou wilt forgive their sin—" break off with a soul-wrenching sob? It appears to do so. And there follows that anguished appeal, "And if not, blot me, I pray thee, out of thy book." It was impossible for Moses to take the consequences for Israel's sin and receive their just punishment. But he offered himself as a substitute. Such selfless love makes this prayer one of the greatest in all the Word of God.

And God did not destroy Israel for the sake of His servant Moses.

Elijah's Prayer on Mount Carmel

Another Old Testament prophet leaves us a prayer of epic proportions in 1 Kings 18:36-37. Elijah is on Mount Carmel. The prophets of Baal have exhausted themselves in pleading to their god to bring down fire upon their sacrifice. But "there was neither voice, nor any to answer, nor any that regarded" (v. 29).

And now at the end of the grueling day, Elijah's turn has come. He repairs the broken-down altar of the Lord, he lays on the wood, he prepares the sacrifice, he drenches it all with water. One thing remains: to make contact with God.

Note the solemn but confident address. "<u>Lord God of Abraham, Isaac, and of Israel, let it be known this day that</u>

thou art God in Israel."

This is his first and foremost petition.

CAN YOU EXPRESS THIS SUBLIME OUTPOURING?

"And that I am thy servant, and that I have done all these things at thy word." His credentials.

Feel the emotion rise as he becomes more importunate.

"Hear me, O Lord, hear me, that this people may know that thou art the Lord God."

Ah! That is the point. This people! Always the people! That they may know and be convinced! They have been halting between two opinions. Is the Lord the God or is Baal the god? Prove to them by a flash of fire that Thou art God, "and that thou hast turned their heart back again."

What a prayer! Its confidence in Jehovah God, its throbbing desire that the people might know even as Elijah knows His power and sovereignty, its sublime faith that God was ready to respond. Are we surprised at the answer?

> Then the fire of the Lord fell, and consumed the burnt sacrifice, and the wood, and the stones, and the dust, and licked up the water that was in the trench.
>
> And when all the people saw it, they fell on their faces: and they said, The Lord, he is the God; the Lord, he is the God (1 Kings 18:38-39).

Jesus' Prayer in Gethsemane

No human prayer can approximate the prayer of Jesus in the Garden of Gethsemane. As we draw near, we must put off our shoes, for we stand on holy ground.

Leaving all but three of the chosen band at the garden gate, He makes His way deeper into the olive grove. He knew what awaited Him there. How plaintive is His request, "My soul is exceeding sorrowful, even unto death: tarry ye here, and watch with me." He desperately needed their support.

Going a little farther, He falls upon His face in agony, uttering words both human and divine, "<u>If it be possible, let this cup pass . . . nevertheless not as I will, but as thou wilt.</u>" Here is supreme abandonment to the Father's will.

Rising to this plane of total commitment, He goes back to the three disciples to find them sleeping.

Twice more He returns to the place of His agony to reaffirm the same prayer. In its reiteration He finds the strength He will need to go to Calvary. And each time as He retraces His steps to His disciples, He finds them heavy with sleep.

Truly He has "trodden the winepress alone; and of the people there was none with" Him (Isa. 63:3). Alone, "he hath borne our griefs, and carried our sorrows" (53:4).

> Then cometh Jesus with them unto a place called Gethsemane, and saith unto the disciples, Sit ye here, while I go and pray yonder.
>
> And he took with him Peter and the two sons of Zebedee, and began to be sorrowful and very heavy.
>
> Then saith he unto them, My soul is exceeding sorrowful, even unto death: tarry ye here, and watch with me.
>
> And he went a little farther, and fell on his face, and prayed, saying, O my Father, if it be possible, let this cup pass from me: nevertheless not as I will, but as thou wilt.
>
> And he cometh unto the disciples, and findeth them asleep, and saith unto Peter, What, could ye not watch with me one hour? . . .
>
> He went away again the second time, and prayed, saying, O my Father, if this cup may not pass away from me, except I drink it, thy will be done.
>
> And he came and found them asleep again: for their eyes were heavy.
>
> And he left them, and went away again, and prayed the third time, saying the same words.

YOU ENTER HERE THE HOLY OF HOLIES

Then cometh he to his disciples, and saith unto them, Sleep on now, and take your rest: behold, the hour is at hand, and the Son of man is betrayed into the hands of sinners (*Matt. 26:36-40, 42-45*).

Paul's Prayer for the Ephesians

The eloquence of Paul the apostle reaches no more lofty plane than that attained in his prayers. Notable among them is the one penned to the Ephesian church found in 3:14-21. Each request rises higher than the one preceding as though he were being lifted to the very gates of heaven.

"I bow my knees." The attitude suggests the urgency and the intensity of his prayer.

Paul voices four great petitions:

1. To be strengthened in the inner man with might, for conflict or for service.

2. To be grounded in faith, rooted in love.

3. To comprehend the magnitude of the love of Christ—its breadth, its length, its depth, its height, experiencing that which transcends the understanding.

4. To be filled with God, the fullness of God, with all the fullness of God. Superlatives!

The conclusion is magnificent. Linking God's omnipotence with our human willingness, he declares that there is no limit to the possibilities of grace.

> For this cause I bow my knees unto the Father of our Lord Jesus Christ,
>
> Of whom the whole family in heaven and earth is named,
>
> That he would grant you, according to the riches of his glory, to be strengthened with might by his Spirit in the inner man;
>
> That Christ may dwell in your hearts by faith; that ye, being rooted and grounded in love,
>
> May be able to comprehend with all saints what is the breadth, and length, and depth, and height;

MEMORIZE IT; REPEAT IT OFTEN; YOU WILL TAKE ON STATURE

And to know the love of Christ, which passeth knowledge, that ye might be filled with all the fulness of God.

Now unto him that is able to do exceeding abundantly above all that we ask or think, according to the power that worketh in us,

Unto him be glory in the church by Christ Jesus throughout all ages, world without end. Amen.

David's Valedictory Prayer

There was music in the soul of King David. It sounded forth in the beautiful psalms that bear his name. It is not surprising that it echoes, too, in his prayers. This is evident in the majestic wording of the lyrical utterance recorded in 1 Chron. 29:10-13. It is a paean of praise, all worship, all adoration. Its rhythms are so compelling that to speak them is almost to sing them. God is magnified as Creator, Owner of all wealth, Dispenser of all good, the All-Glorious, worthy of all praise.

Blessed be thou, Lord God of Israel our father, for ever and ever.

Thine, O Lord, is the greatness, and the power, and the glory, and the victory, and the majesty: for all that is in the heaven and in the earth is thine; thine is the kingdom, O Lord, and thou art exalted as head above all.

Both riches and honour come of thee, and thou reignest over all; and in thine hand is power and might, and in thine hand it is to make great, and to give strength unto all.

Now therefore, our God, we thank thee, and praise thy glorious name.

The Great Benedictions

Among the epic passages in the Word of God the benedictions must be noted. Their language is lofty, and their expressions of goodwill and felicity lift one to a height of sublime revelation.

The voice will be strong and energized. There will be a lilt in the rhythm. A benediction is almost a hymn, a song of trust and confidence and union. Most benedictions are poems. Feel brotherly love as well as love for God as you repeat the lovely words. They are uplifting, inspiring, ennobling. They imply,

"To God be the glory!"
"Till we meet again!"
"Keep the faith!"

A benediction is usually considered as a pronouncement of final blessing. But the biblical benedictions are far more than the perfunctory closure of a letter or an interview or an occasion. They come as a spontaneous invoking of affection and love that refreshes the spirit and bathes the soul in a flood of joy and praise. They are often preceded by anxiously worded advice or admonition.

Such is the benediction with which Peter closes his first letter to the strangers scattered throughout the Gentile world. He first makes pointed suggestions to the elders regarding their ministry. Feed the flock willingly, not for the money involved, not arrogantly, but as an example, as a shepherd.

He then has a word for the flock, of submission one to another, of humility, of freedom from corroding care, of sobriety, of awareness of the wiles of the tempter.

Then he launches into his final word, a benediction of such quality and depth that it has become a model for the use of all who minister.

The God of all grace,
Who hath called us unto his eternal glory by Christ Jesus,
After that ye have suffered a while,
Make you perfect,
  stablish,
    strengthen,
      settle you.

THE BENEDICTION IS THE CLIMAX. MAKE IT SO!

To him be glory and dominion for ever and ever. Amen *(1 Pet. 5:10-11).*

He is full of grace! Grace to meet every human need! Grace to forgive, to purify, to sustain, and to keep in perfect peace.

And through the redemption provided by Christ's sacrificial death, He has called us to share eternal glory with Him. What a prospect!

But before that, while we are yet in these bodies, we shall be called upon to suffer. This is to demonstrate His grace, to prove our fidelity to Him, to deepen our dependence on Him, to make us more sympathetic with other sufferers, to identify us more completely with Jesus himself, who, "that he might sanctify the people with his own blood, suffered without the gate" (Heb. 13:12).

There is a mystery in human suffering, but suffering is inevitable. It may not be physical. Mental, emotional, and spiritual anguish can transcend pain of body. Suffering is a test. If we can pass it victoriously, we shall find it a means of perfecting, strengthening, and stabilizing us. And it is "for a while." We are assured that He knows the measure of our endurance, and He will never give us more than we can bear (1 Cor. 10:13).

And when as "more than conquerors" (Rom. 8:37) we stand exultantly before Him *now* and *then*, we are and shall be ready to ascribe to Him all "glory and dominion for ever and ever. Amen." This is the only possible climax to such a benediction.

Another familiar and favorite benediction is found in the Old Testament in Num. 6:24-26. This is a model blessing given by Moses to Aaron and his sons with which they in turn were to bless the children of Israel.

> The Lord bless thee, and keep thee:
>
> The Lord make his face shine upon thee, and be gracious unto thee:
>
> The Lord lift up his countenance upon thee, and give thee peace.

"<u>The Lord bless thee</u>"; that is, protect you from harm; "<u>and keep thee</u>"; that is, continually and permanently extend to you His watch care.

"<u>The Lord make his face shine upon thee</u>"; that is, keep looking your way so that you have ever in view the radiance of His smile; "<u>be gracious unto thee</u>"; the plea is, though His favor is undeserved, that it may be extended anyhow so that you bask in the warmth of His presence.

"<u>The Lord lift up his countenance upon thee</u>"; that is, may He give you His full attention and His unremitting love. We cannot understand how the Almighty God who has created and who keeps the universe operating can have concern for one of the least of His children. But we know that He does. We are enjoined to "come boldly unto the throne of grace, that we may obtain mercy, and find grace to help in time of need" (Heb. 4:16).

So unashamedly we can voice this petition, knowing that He will answer and furthermore give to His trusting servants the prize of peace. This peace is not only the rest of tranquility, but total well-being.

Another great benediction is found in Jude 24-25. This, as some of the others, is preceded immediately by words of extreme warning against the ungodly, the murmurers, the complainers, the bigots, the sensuous, the arrogant.

Then comes the mighty transition. "<u>But ye, beloved, building up yourselves on your most holy faith, praying in the Holy Ghost, keep yourselves in the love of God, looking for the mercy of our Lord Jesus Christ unto eternal life</u>" (vv. 20-21).

You are different. You need not succumb to the pressures of your day and generation. Through your conscientious growth in grace, through prayer, through your steadfast purpose to be true, through God's great grace, you can win. And now feel the tremendous support and promise of these strong words:

> Unto him that is able to keep you from falling, and to present you faultless before the presence of his glory with exceeding joy,
>
> To the only wise God our Saviour, be glory and majesty, dominion and power, both now and ever. Amen.

LIFT THE HEARERS WITH THESE MIGHTY WORDS

Aware of the perils of this Christian way, Jude still confidently declares that we need never fall. God is so mighty that if we put our trust in Him, we can stand before Him to be judged with no "errors" charged against us, no "penalties" for stumbling or faltering, no "demerits" to affect our score. We shall be without fault. And having heard His "well done," our joy shall know no bounds. One translation has it, we shall be "wild with joy."

Such an accomplishment calls for an outpouring of praise to God, the only God, the only wise God, to God, our Savior, made our Savior through His identity with Jesus, the Redeemer, to Him be glory and majesty, dominion and power.

What a piling of superlatives! Resplendence, grandeur, sovereignty, total control, and unbelievable might. These are His attributes, and He has promised to keep us! Now and ever. Amen and Amen.

A short but very meaningful benediction is found in 1 Tim. 1:17. As Paul contemplated again his own remarkable conversion, he says:

> I obtained mercy, that in me first Jesus Christ might shew forth all longsuffering, for a pattern to them which should hereafter believe on him to life everlasting (v. 16).

Then there leapt from his pen words of exultant beauty.

> Now unto the King eternal, immortal, invisible, the only wise God, be honour and glory for ever and ever. Amen.

The King eternal, without beginning or ending, everlasting; immortal, divine, infinite; invisible, a Spirit, a Presence without human form, beyond human comprehension:

"To Him, the only God, be honor and glory world without end."

Memorize it, preachers, and use it. It will be more appropriate and exalted than any closing prayer you may compose.

The burst of praise found in 1 Tim. 6:15-16 does not come as a *final* benediction. Paul has been alerting his son in the gospel, the "man of God," to beware of false teachers, to avoid the subtle danger of riches, to be content with his station in life, to fight the good fight of faith that at the appearing of Jesus he might be found without blame. And the very contemplation of the second coming of the Lord, like a match striking dry wood, causes a burst of holy flame; he adoringly writes of

> The blessed and only Potentate,
> The King of kings, and Lord of lords;
>
> Who only hath immortality,
> Dwelling in the light which no man can approach unto;
> Whom no man hath seen, nor can see:
> To whom be honour and power everlasting. Amen.

BATHE YOUR SOUL IN MAJESTY

Paul strengthens and fortifies his estimate of Jesus by his strong negation. The *only* Potentate; who *only* hath immortality; *no* man can approach His dazzling brightness; *no* man hath seen, nor can see, Him. He is exclusive in His greatness; He is superlative in His power. He is *the* Potentate.

And for a final example of a great benediction, let us look at Heb. 13:20-21.

> Now the God of peace, that brought again from the dead our Lord Jesus, that great shepherd of the sheep, through the blood of the everlasting covenant,
>
> Make you perfect in every good work to do his will, working in you that which is wellpleasing in his sight, through Jesus Christ; to whom be glory for ever and ever. Amen.

One sentence of 59 words! They must be broken up into phrases if we are to read them with effect, much less have breath enough to do so.

The words are sublime. Yet there is a practicality, a sensing of personal accountability in these words that makes this prayer unique. Not only is God Almighty worthy of honor and praise; but because of the Lamb slain from the foundation of the world for our redemption, we have a debt to pay, the debt of a life made perfect in His sight.

Refreshing, too, is the salutation to the God of peace. There was enmity between God and man. Sin made an irreconcilable difference between us. But our Lord Jesus, who died, was buried, and rose again, tasting death for every man, has restored peace between man and God through the shedding of His own precious blood— the Blood of the everlasting covenant.

HE IS THE AUTHOR OF OUR SALVATION

The writer of these matchless words does not stumble at the thought of man's perfection before God. Boldly he expressed the wish and the prayer that we should be made perfect in every good work <u>to do His will</u>. That is the point! Perfect subjection to His will; perfect obedience to His law.

And this makes us well pleasing to Him. But it is only through Jesus Christ, the great Shepherd of the sheep. A tender reference. "All we like sheep have gone astray; we have turned every one to his own way" (Isa. 53:6); "but [we] are now returned unto the Shepherd and Bishop of [our] souls" (1 Pet. 2:25).

Are you impressed with those words with which most of the benedictions have closed: "for ever and ever"? In this world of change and decay, of the rise and fall of nations, think of a kingdom that is permanent and everlasting, which shall never become corrupt and never be overthrown. It is forever and forever! Hallelujah!

> *Crowns and thrones may perish,*
> *Kingdoms rise and wane;*
> *But the Church of Jesus*
> *Constant will remain.*
> *Gates of hell can never*
> *'Gainst that Church prevail;*
> *We have Christ's own promise,*
> *Which can never fail.*
>
> Refrain:
> *Onward, Christian soldiers! . . .*
>
> —SABINE BARING-GOULD

The Seven Last Words of Jesus

How could we more fittingly close this chapter and this book than with a reference to the seven last words of Jesus. C. H. Spurgeon has called them "The Cries from the Cross." An attempt to convey their depth of meaning orally will challenge the ability and the understanding of every reader and will provide a lifetime assignment in excellence.

To even attempt to reproduce His spirit as He uttered these words seems almost a sacrilege. Yet the great apostle has enjoined us, "Let this mind be in you, which was also in Christ Jesus" (Phil. 2:5). How can we better partake of His life than by repeatedly climbing Calvary's hill to there relive the scene of His atonement for us. How can we better know the obedience of His death than by repeating the words that accompanied it.

These last words are not found in their entirety in any one Gospel. But it does no violence to the truth to arrange them in time sequence as they were no doubt uttered.

The first word is found in Luke 23:34:

Father, forgive them; for they know not what they do.

The most godlike quality of which man is capable is his ability to forgive. Paradoxically enough, it is the one condition upon which man himself can be forgiven of God—that he forgive his fellowmen.

Forgiveness is not based upon deserving. Those for whom Christ prayed on the Cross did not deserve His forgiveness. Not the mob who had been shouting, "Crucify him"; not the soldiers who drove the nails; not the scribes and Pharisees who had schemed for His death; not Pilate who condemned Him, nor Judas who betrayed Him, nor Peter who denied Him; not the disciples who forsook Him. Certainly all of us for whom He died did not deserve forgiveness. But He prayed for them and for us, "<u>Father, forgive them</u>." And because He prayed this prayer, God can forgive us.

The Greek justifies the translation, "Jesus kept on saying, '<u>Father, forgive them</u>.'" As though with every blow of the hammers He reiterated His petition. Your voice can suggest the intensity of His plea.

The second clause demands our attention. "<u>They know not what they do</u>." It is easier to forgive if one can bring himself to this magnanimous point of view. It is a lofty one—far removed from thoughts of retaliation or spite or vindictiveness. It is easier to attribute wrong and destructive conduct to hatred, jealousy, malice, envy, strife. But Jesus is saying, They are ignorant, they do not understand, they do not realize. Forgive them! They do not know I am dying for them. These beautiful words must be spoken with infinite compassion and infinite love.

The second word is found in Luke 23:43:

<u>To day shalt thou be with me in paradise</u>.

Picture the scene. The Son of glory hanging on a cross between two thieves suspended on crosses. See the agony on their faces, watch them writhe in pain, hear their cries of anguish and despair.

RELIVE THE CALVARY SCENE

One of the malefactors railed on Jesus, slurring His divinity—"If thou be Christ, save thyself and us."

But the other thief rebuked him, confessing the justice of their punishment and the innocence of Jesus. Then addressing the Master, he said, "Lord, remember me when thou comest into thy kingdom." Here was recognition of His Messiahship and a plea for mercy.

It received an immediate response. "Today—when death has done its work—today you shall join Me in paradise."

The Savior is speaking now. He came to buy back everyone sold into sin. He was even then paying redemption's price. This dying thief was His first trophy. His response was unconditional. No long confession, no required acts of retribution. He recognized penitence and rewarded it graciously.

This was what He had come to do. Read it with assurance.

The third word is found in John 19:26-27:

<u>Woman, behold thy son! Behold thy mother!</u>

This tender word moves us deeply. In the midst of His agony and shame, Jesus looks down from the Cross and sees His mother standing beside His closest earthly friend, John the Beloved, the only one of His disciples who had not forsaken Him.

His mother! It was she who had heard the angel's amazing words more than 33 years before that she had been chosen to bear the Christ, the God-man, the Messiah. Her response had been, "Behold the handmaid of the Lord; be it unto me according to thy word" (Luke 1:38).

EXQUISITE TENDERNESS AND LOVE

The prophecy that a sword should pierce through her own soul (Luke 2:35) was now being fulfilled. Her anguish must have been second only to that of the Lord himself. And Jesus, knowing these things, responded with an unforgettable legacy. He gave John to her as a son. He gave her to John as a mother. It was His last will and testament. He had no property to leave her. The soldiers were even then gambling for His seamless robe. But He had an abundance of love and thoughtfulness to leave to them both.

What unspeakable comfort this must have brought to these grief-stricken loved ones! And they accepted the gift of Christ's love, for the Word declares, "From that hour that disciple took her unto his own home."

What compassion is required for the reading of these emotion-packed lines.

The fourth word:

My God, my God, why hast thou forsaken me? *(Matt. 27:46).*

This cry strikes terror to every believing heart. The withdrawal of the Divine Presence is the thing most to be dreaded by every devout soul.

More than any other of Jesus' last words, this probably represents the extent of the price He must pay to effect our redemption. He in this moment tasted death for every man. He knew the darkness that engulfs a lost soul. He bore the full load of human sin, which is total separation from God. He was divine, and He knew that weight of the burden He had willingly assumed. But He was also human, and from His anguished lips came the cry, "Why?" "He hath made him to be sin for us, who knew no sin; that we might be made the righteousness of God in him" (2 Cor. 5:21).

In Gethsemane He had prayed, "Father, if thou be willing, remove this cup from me: nevertheless not my will, but thine, be done" (Luke 22:42). This is the cup, and He drinks it to its last bitter dregs. He suffers for the moment God's judgment upon sin. He bore our iniquities (cf. Isa. 53:11).

REALIZE THE DEPTH OF THE SACRIFICE

The despairing cry was *My* God. In the darkness that engulfed His spirit, He felt the alienation from His Father's infinite love. But He was tasting death for every man. "Eli, Eli, lama sabachthani?"

The fifth word, John 19:28:

I thirst.

This is a human cry. His suffering body craved a drink. In all points He was "touched with the feeling of our infirmities"; He was such an one "as we are, yet without sin" (Heb. 4:15). This cry reveals the total identification of God with man. The biblical account seems to indicate that Christ was offered two drinks. The first He refused because it was a sedative, and He did not wish to deaden the pain of His excruciating suffering on our behalf.

He drank the cup—all of it.

HE WAS HUMAN; WE IDENTIFY

The second drink, which He accepted, was given by an unknown soldier who probably offered the sour beverage he himself had been rationed. In the angry mob, full of hatred, that surrounded the crucified Lord, he stands alone, a symbol of compassion. Saturating a sponge with the drink, he extended it to Jesus upon the long stalk of a hyssop plant and pressed it against the burning lips of the Master; Christ was thus able to draw the liquid from the sponge and quench His thirst.

At Sychar's well He had been thirsty, too, and there a profligate woman was the one who ministered to His need. She was a Samaritan, but He introduced her to the living water. And now a Roman soldier answers His cry for drink. Let us hope he, too, found the life-giving stream. Both will ever remain nameless; but they declare that Jesus, Son of God and Son of Man, belonged not to the Jewish race alone but to all mankind.

He knew physical thirst, and so He could declare, "If any man thirst, let him come unto me, and drink" (John 7:37).

"Ho, every one that thirsteth, come ye to the waters" (Isa. 55:1).

The sixth word:

It is finished *(John 19:30).*

Jesus declared: "I lay down my life, that I might take it again. No man taketh it from me, but I lay it down of myself. I have power to lay it down, and I have power to take it again. This commandment have I received of my Father" (John 10:17-18).   **OMNIPOTENCE**

Jesus was not a victim! He is a victor! For three hours He endured the pangs of death that He might bring life and immortality to all men. Now looking up into His Father's face, He receives the divine approbation that outraged justice has been satisfied. His redemptive work is complete. With triumph and with finality He cries, "It is finished."

This may well be the most significant word uttered in all the history of the race of men. (It is one word in the original.) Christ did not stop short of the fulfillment of redemption's plan. Not in Gethsemane, not in Caiaphas' hall, nor before Pilate, not as He struggled up Calvary's hill, nor when He hung suspended on the cruel Cross. Not until the Father said, "It is enough," did He lay down His life.

Let His repeated words become for us a vow of our own fidelity. May we so live that with Him we can daily say, "I have finished the work which thou gavest me to do" (John 17:4).

The seventh word:

Father, into thy hands I commend my spirit *(Luke 23:46).*

This is indeed a benediction. What confidence it expresses; what calm assurance it implies; what perfect oneness with the Father it presupposes.

His earthly mission accomplished, He passes back into the eternity from which He came to be ever at the right hand of the Father.

These words are a direct quotation from David in Ps. 31:5: "Into thine hand I commit my spirit: thou hast redeemed me, O Lord God of truth."

May we, too, be able to say this when our lifework is done: "Into thy hands I commend my spirit."

What a safe abiding place! What a refuge when the conflict on earth is done! What a haven of rest!

This is an affirmation of the oneness existing between the Father and the Son. Coexistent, coequal, coeternal.

APPENDIX

Arrangements of Scripture Passages for Special Occasions

All the selections are for the most part from the King James Version and have been edited by the author for ease in oral reading.

A Candlelight Installation Service

Send out thy light and thy truth: let them lead me. God is light, and in him is no darkness at all. God so loved the world, that he [sent] his only begotten Son. In him was life; and the life was the light of men. [He] was the true Light, which lighteth every man that cometh into the world.

Jesus [declared of himself], I am the light of the world: he that followeth me shall not walk in darkness, but shall have the light of life.

God, who commanded the light to shine out of darkness, hath shined in our hearts, to give the light of the knowledge of the glory of God in the face of Jesus Christ. Ye were sometimes darkness, but now are ye light in the Lord. Ye are a chosen generation . . . that ye should shew forth the praises of him who hath called you out of darkness into his marvellous light. Bear witness of the Light, that all men through him might believe.

[Jesus said,] Ye are the light of the world. A city that is set on an hill cannot be hid. Neither do men light a candle, and put it under a bushel, but on a candlestick; and it giveth light unto all that are in the house. Let your light so shine before men, that they may see your good works, and glorify your Father which is in heaven.

Arise, shine; for thy light is come, and the glory of the Lord is risen upon thee. . . . darkness shall cover the earth, and gross darkness the people: but the Lord shall arise upon thee, and his glory shall be seen upon thee.

Ye are all the children of light. Walk as children of light.

Taken from: Ps. 43:3; 1 John 1:5; John 3:16; 1:4, 9; 8:12; 2 Cor. 4:6; Eph. 5:8*a*; 1 Pet. 2:9; John 1:7; Matt. 5:14-16; Isa. 60:1-2; 1 Thess. 5:5; Eph. 5:8*b*

Admonitions to Teachers

[Hear the Word of the Lord, spoken to Moses, His servant, and to others.]

O Israel: The Lord our God is one Lord: and thou shalt love the Lord thy God with all thine heart, and with all thy soul, and with all thy might. And these words, which I command thee this day, shall be in thine heart: and thou shalt teach them diligently unto thy children, and shalt talk of them when thou sittest in thine house, and when thou walkest by the way, and when thou liest down, and when thou risest up.

Know therefore that the Lord thy God, he is God, the faithful God, which keepeth covenant and mercy with them that love him and keep his commandments to a thousand generations.

Only fear the Lord, and serve him in truth with all your heart: for consider how great things he hath done for you.

We are bound to give thanks alway to God for you, brethren beloved of the Lord, because God hath from the beginning chosen you to salvation through sanctification of the Spirit and belief of the truth: whereunto he called you by our gospel, to the obtaining of the glory of our Lord Jesus Christ. Therefore, brethren, stand fast, and hold the traditions which ye have been taught.

Let the word of Christ dwell in you richly in all wisdom; teaching and admonishing one another in psalms and hymns and spiritual songs, singing with grace in your hearts to the Lord.

Having then gifts differing according to the grace that is given to us, whether prophecy, let us prophesy according to the proportion of faith; or ministry, let us wait on our ministering: or he that teacheth, on teaching.

Be thou an example of the believers, in word, in conversation, in charity, in spirit, in faith, in purity. Give attendance to reading, to exhortation, to doctrine.

Meditate upon these things; give thyself wholly to them; that thy profiting may appear to all. Take heed unto thyself, and unto the doctrine; continue in them: for in doing this thou shalt both save thyself, and them that hear thee.

We also do not cease to pray for you, and to desire that ye might be filled with the knowledge of his will in all wisdom and spiritual understanding; that ye might walk worthy of the Lord unto all pleasing, being fruitful in every good work, and increasing in the knowledge of God; strengthened with all might, according to his glorious power, unto all patience and longsuffering with joyfulness, . . . warning every man, and teaching every man in all wisdom; that we may present every man perfect in Christ Jesus.

Our Lord Jesus Christ himself, and God, even our Father, which hath loved us, and hath given us everlasting consolation and good hope through grace, comfort your hearts, and stablish you in every good word and work.

Now unto him that is able to do exceeding abundantly above all that we ask or think, according to the power that worketh in us, unto him be glory in the church by Christ Jesus throughout all ages, world without end. Amen.

Taken from: Deut. 6:4-7; 7:9; 1 Sam. 12:24; 2 Thess. 2:13-15; Col. 3:16; Rom. 12:6-7; 1 Tim. 4:12-13, 15-16; Col. 1:9-11, 28; 2 Thess. 2:16-17; Eph. 3:20-21

The Pastor's Valedictory to His Church

Christ also loved the church, and gave himself for it; that he might sanctify and cleanse it with the washing of water by the word, that he might present it to himself a glorious church, not having spot, or wrinkle, or any such thing; but that it should be holy and without blemish.

Therefore, my brethren dearly beloved, so stand fast in the Lord.

Rejoice in the Lord alway: and again I say, Rejoice. Let your moderation be known unto all men. The Lord is at hand. Be careful for nothing; but in every thing by prayer and supplication with thanksgiving let your requests be made known unto God. And the peace of God, which passeth all understanding, shall keep your hearts and minds through Christ Jesus.

Finally, brethren, whatsoever things are true, whatsoever things are honest, whatsoever things are just, whatsoever things are pure, whatsoever things are lovely, whatsoever things are of good report; if there be any virtue, and if there be any praise, think on these things. Those things, which ye have both learned and received, and heard, and seen in me, do: and the God of peace shall be with you.

And I, brethren, when I came to you, determined not to know any thing among you, save Jesus Christ, and him crucified. And my speech and my preaching was not with enticing words of man's wisdom, but in demonstration of the Spirit and of power: that your faith should not stand in the wisdom of men, but in the power of God.

And now, brethren, I commend you to God, and to the word of his grace, which is able to build you up, and to give you an inheritance among all them which are sanctified.

Taken from: Eph. 5:25-27; Phil. 4:1, 4-9; 1 Cor. 2:1-2, 4-5; Acts 20:32

The Church's Response to the Departing Pastor

For this cause I bow my knees unto the Father of our Lord Jesus Christ, of whom the whole family in heaven and earth is named, that he would grant you, according to the riches of his glory, to be strengthened with might by his Spirit in the inner man; that Christ may dwell in your hearts by faith; that ye, being rooted and grounded in love, may be able to comprehend with all saints what is the breadth, and length, and depth, and height; and to know the love of Christ, which passeth knowledge, that ye might be filled with all the fulness of God.

Now unto him that is able to do exceeding abundantly above all that we ask or think, according to the power that worketh in us, unto him be glory in the church by Christ Jesus throughout all ages, world without end.

The Lord bless thee, and keep thee:

The Lord make his face shine upon thee, and be gracious unto thee:

The Lord lift up his countenance upon thee, and give thee peace.

Taken from: Eph. 3:14-21; Num. 6:24-26

The Uplifted Christ

[The children of Israel] journeyed from mount Hor by the way of the Red sea, to compass the land of Edom: and the soul of the people was much discouraged because of the way.

And the people spake against God, and against Moses, Wherefore have ye brought us up out of Egypt to die in the wilderness? for there is no bread, neither is there any water; and our soul loatheth this light bread [manna].

And the Lord sent fiery serpents among the people, and they bit the people; and much people of Israel died.

Therefore the people came to Moses, and said, We have sinned, for we have spoken against the Lord, and against thee; pray unto the Lord, that he take away the serpents from us. And Moses prayed for the people.

And the Lord said unto Moses, Make thee a fiery serpent, and set it upon a pole: and it shall come to pass, that every one that is bitten, when he looketh upon it, shall live.

And Moses made a serpent of brass, and put it upon a pole, and it came to pass, that if a serpent had bitten any man, when he beheld the serpent of brass, he lived.

[And Jesus said,] As Moses lifted up the serpent in the wilderness, even so must the Son of man be lifted up: that whosoever believeth in him should not perish, but have eternal life.

And I, if I be lifted up from the earth, will draw all men unto me. This he said, signifying what death he should die.

He became obedient unto death, even the death of the cross. Wherefore God also hath highly exalted him, and given him a name which is above every name: that at the name of Jesus every knee should bow . . . and that every tongue should confess that Jesus Christ is Lord, to the glory of God the Father.

Then said Jesus unto his disciples, If any man will come after me, let him deny himself, and take up his cross, and follow me.

Except a corn of wheat fall into the ground and die, it abideth alone: but if it die, it bringeth forth much fruit.

He that loveth his life shall lose it; and he that hateth his life in this world shall keep it unto life eternal.

If any man serve me, let him follow me.

Always bearing about in the body the dying of the Lord Jesus.

[For if He be lifted up in our lives, dead to self but alive unto God, He will draw all men unto Him.]

Taken from: Num. 21:4-9; John 3:14-15; 12:32-33; Phil. 2:8-11; Matt. 16:24; John 12:24-26; 2 Cor. 4:10

God's Commandments

The Lord called unto [Moses] out of [Mount Sinai], saying, Thus shalt thou say to the house of Jacob, and tell the children of Israel; I bare you on eagles' wings, and brought you unto myself. Now therefore, if ye will obey my voice indeed, and keep my covenant, then ye shall be a peculiar treasure unto me above all people. These are the words which thou shalt speak unto the children of Israel.

Thou shalt have no other gods before me.

Thou shalt not make unto thee any graven image.

Thou shalt not take the name of the Lord thy God in vain.

Remember the sabbath day, to keep it holy.

Honour thy father and thy mother.

Thou shalt not kill.

Thou shalt not commit adultery.

Thou shalt not steal.

Thou shalt not bear false witness.

Thou shalt not covet.

Hear, O Israel: The Lord our God is one Lord: and thou shalt love the Lord thy God with all thine heart, and with all thy soul, and with all thy might. And these words, which I command thee this day, shall be in thine heart; and thou shalt teach them diligently unto thy children, and shalt talk of them when thou sittest in thine house, and when thou walkest by the way, and when thou liest down, and when thou risest up.

When the Lord thy God shall give thee great and goodly cities, which thou buildedst not, and houses full of all good things, которые thou filledst not, when thou shalt have eaten and be full; then <u>beware lest thou forget the Lord</u>.

I call heaven and earth to record this day against you, that I have set before you life and death, blessing and cursing: therefore choose life, that both thou and thy [children] may live: that thou mayest love the Lord thy God, and that thou mayest obey his voice: for he is thy life[!]

> Taken from: Exod. 19:3-6; 20:3-4, 7-8, 12-17; Deut. 6:4-7, 10-12; 30:19-20

Stewardship

Moses ordained the tithe.

All the tithe of the land, whether of the seed of the land, or of the fruit of the tree, is the Lord's: it is holy unto the Lord.

Solomon reaffirmed its validity.

Honour the Lord with thy substance, and with the firstfruits of all thine increase: so shall thy barns be filled with plenty, and thy presses shall burst out with new wine.

Malachi located the failure to pay tithe as a cause of backsliding.

[Hear this dialogue:] I am the Lord, I change not. Even from the days of your fathers ye are gone away from mine ordinances, and have not kept them. Return unto me, and I will return unto you . . .

But ye said, Wherein shall we return?

Will a man rob God? Yet ye have robbed me.

But ye say, Wherein have we robbed thee?

In tithes and offerings. . . .

Bring ye all the tithes into the storehouse, that there may be meat in mine house, and prove me now herewith, saith the Lord of hosts, if I will not open you the windows of heaven, and pour you out a blessing, that there shall not be room enough to receive it.

Paul reaffirms the blessed results of liberality.

As ye abound in every thing, in faith, and utterance, and knowledge, and in all diligence, and in your love to us, see that ye abound in this grace also. For ye know the grace of our Lord Jesus Christ, that, though he was rich, yet for your sakes he became poor, that ye through his poverty might be rich.

He which soweth sparingly shall reap also sparingly; and he which soweth bountifully shall reap also bountifully. Every man according as he purposeth in his heart, so let him give; not grudgingly, or of necessity: for God loveth a cheerful giver.

And God is able to make all grace abound toward you; that ye, always having all sufficiency in all things, may abound to every good work; . . . being enriched in every thing to all bountifulness, which causeth through us thanksgiving to God.

Taken from: Lev. 27:30; Prov. 3:9-10; Mal. 3:6-8, 10; 2 Cor. 8:7, 9; 9:6-8, 11

Give Me This Mountain

Introduction:

The miraculous deliverance from Pharaoh, king of Egypt, had been effected. The long wilderness journey was over. And now at last the children of Israel were ready to enter the Promised Land.

Twelve spies were sent in to explore Canaan and to bring back a report. Forty days later they returned, unanimous in declaring it to be a good land flowing with milk and honey. But 10 of them reported that the cities were great and walled and that giants possessed the land. Of the whole committee, only Caleb and Joshua declared that the children of Israel were able to go in and possess their promised inheritance. The majority report prevailed, and the people turned back to wilderness wanderings.

God in His wrath swore that none of those whose hearts failed them for fear should see the Promised Land. And it was so.

But now, 45 years later, Caleb the son of Jephunneh came unto Joshua, the successor of Moses, and reminded him of "the thing that the Lord said unto Moses the man of God concerning me and thee in Kadesh-barnea.

"Forty years old was I when Moses sent me [to spy] out the land; and I brought him word again as it was in mine heart, [saying,] Let us go up at once, and possess it; for we are well able to overcome it.

"Nevertheless my brethren that went up with me [said], We be not able to go up, for there we saw the giants [in the land]: and we were in our own sight as grasshoppers.

"[And they] made the heart of the [children of Israel] melt: but I wholly followed the Lord my God.

"And God said, Surely [this people] shall not see the land which I sware unto their fathers, neither shall any of them that provoked me see it: but my servant Caleb, because he had another spirit with him, and hath followed me fully, him will I bring into the land whereinto he went; and his seed shall possess it.

"And now," Caleb said unto Joshua, "behold, the Lord hath kept me alive these forty and five years, while the children of Israel wandered in the wilderness: and now, lo, I am this day fourscore and five years old. As yet I am as strong this day as I was in the day that Moses sent me: as my strength was then, even so is my strength now, for war, both to go out, and to come in.

"Now therefore give me this mountain, whereof the Lord spake in that day; for thou heardest how the Anakims were there, and that the cities were great and fenced: if so be the Lord will be with me, then I shall be able to drive them out, as the Lord said."

"And Joshua blessed him, and gave unto Caleb the son of Jephunneh Hebron for an inheritance . . . because that he wholly followed the Lord God of Israel." And Caleb drove out the sons of Anak, and he took the mountain.

Taken from Joshua 14—15 and Numbers 13—14

David and Goliath

The Philistines gathered together their armies to battle. And Saul and the men of Israel were arrayed against them.

And there went a champion out of the camp of the Philistines, named Goliath, whose height was six cubits and a span. He had a helmet of brass upon his head, and he was armed with a coat of mail. And the staff of his spear was like a weaver's beam.

And he stood and cried unto the armies of Israel, "Why are ye come out to set your battle in array? Choose you a man for you, and let him come down to me. If he be able to fight with me, and to kill me, then will we be your servants: but if I prevail against him, and kill him, then shall ye be our servants. I *defy* the armies of Israel this day."

When Saul and all Israel heard those words of the Philistine, they were dismayed, and greatly afraid.

Now Jesse, the Israelite, had eight sons. David, the youngest, kept his father's sheep, and the three eldest followed Saul. And Jesse said unto David, "Take now for thy brethren an ephah of this parched corn, and these ten loaves, and carry these ten cheeses unto the captain of the army, and look how thy brethren fare."

And David rose up early in the morning and came to the camp, and ran into the army, and saluted his brethren. And as he talked with them, behold, there came up the champion, the Philistine of Gath, Goliath by name. And he shouted his challenge to Israel.

And David said, "Who is this uncircumcised Philistine, that he would defy the armies of the living God?" And when the words were heard which David spake, they rehearsed them before Saul; and he sent for him.

And David said to Saul, "Let no man's heart fail because of him; thy servant will go and fight with this Philistine." And Saul said to David, "Thou art but a youth, and he a man of war." And David said unto Saul, "Thy servant kept his father's sheep, and there came a lion, and a bear, and took a lamb out of the flock: and I went out after them and slew them. And this Philistine shall be as one of them, seeing he hath defied the armies of the living God. The Lord will deliver me out of the hand of this Philistine." And Saul said unto David, "Go, and the Lord be with thee."

And he took his staff in his hand, and chose him five smooth stones out of the brook, and put them in a shepherd's bag which he had, and his sling was in his hand: and he drew near to the Philistine.

And when Goliath saw David, he disdained him and said, "Am I a dog, that thou comest to me with staves?" And he cursed David by his gods and said, "Come to me, and I will give thy flesh unto the fowls of the air, and to the beasts of the field."

Then said David to the Philistine, "Thou comest to me with a sword, and with a spear; but I come to thee in the name of the Lord of hosts, the God of the armies of Israel, whom thou hast defied. This day will the Lord deliver thee into mine hand . . . And all this assembly shall know that the Lord saveth not with sword and spear: for the battle is the Lord's."

And it came to pass that David put his hand in his bag, and took thence a stone, and slang it, and smote Goliath, and the stone sank into his forehead; and he fell upon his face to the earth.

So David prevailed over the giant. And when the Philistines saw their champion was dead, they fled.

1 Sam. 17:1-51, abridged

In the Fiery Furnace

Nebuchadnezzar the king made an image of gold and set it up in the plain of Dura, in the province of Babylon.

Then an herald cried aloud, "To you it is commanded, O people, that at what time ye hear the sound of music, ye fall down and worship the golden image that Nebuchadnezzar the king hath set up: and whoso falleth not down and worshippeth shall the same hour be cast into the midst of a burning fiery furnace."

Therefore at that time, when all the people heard the sound of music, all fell down and worshipped the golden image.

Wherefore at that time certain Chaldeans came near and said, "There are certain Jews, Shadrach, Meshach, and Abednego, who have not regarded thee: they serve not thy gods nor worship the golden image which thou hast set up."

Then Nebuchadnezzar in his rage and fury commanded to bring Shadrach, Meshach, and Abednego. "Is it true, do not ye serve my gods, nor worship the golden image which I have set up?" They answered and said, "O Nebuchadnezzar, we are not careful to answer thee in this matter. If it be so, our God whom we serve is able to deliver us from the burning fiery furnace, and he will deliver us. But if not, be it known unto thee, O king, that we will not serve thy gods, nor worship the golden image which thou hast set up."

Then these men were bound in their coats, their hose, and their hats, and their other garments, and were cast into the midst of the burning fiery furnace. Because the king's commandment was urgent, and the furnace exceeding hot, the flame of the fire slew those men that took up Shadrach, Meshach, and Abednego.

Then Nebuchadnezzar the king was astonished, and rose up in haste, and said unto his counsellors, "Did not we cast three men bound into the midst of the fire? Lo, I see four men loose, walking in the midst of the fire, and they have no hurt; and the form of the fourth is like the Son of God."

Then Nebuchadnezzar came near and said, "Ye servants of the most high God, come forth and come hither." And they came forth from the midst of the fire. The princes, governors, and captains, and the king's counsellors, being gathered together, saw these men, upon whose bodies the fire had no power, nor was an hair of their head singed, neither were their coats changed, nor the smell of fire had passed on them.

Then Nebuchadnezzar said, "Blessed be the God of Shadrach, Meshach, and Abednego, who hath sent his angel, and delivered his servants that trusted in him, and have changed the king's word, and yielded their bodies, that they might not serve nor worship any god, except their own God."

Daniel 3, abridged

The Redeemer Cometh

Comfort ye, comfort ye my people, saith your God. Speak ye comfortably to Jerusalem, and cry unto her, that her warfare is accomplished, that her iniquity is pardoned: for she hath received of the Lord's hand double for all her sins. The voice of him that crieth in the wilderness, Prepare ye the way of the Lord, make straight in the desert a highway for our God. Every valley shall be exalted, and every mountain and hill shall be made low: and the crooked shall be made straight, and the rough places plain; and the glory of the Lord shall be revealed, and all flesh shall see it together: for the mouth of the Lord hath spoken it.

Arise, shine; for thy light is come, and the glory of the Lord is risen upon thee. For, behold, the darkness shall cover the earth, and gross darkness the people: but the Lord shall arise upon thee, and his glory shall be seen upon thee. And the Gentiles shall come to thy light, and kings to the brightness of thy rising.

And there shall come forth a rod out of the stem of Jesse, and a Branch shall grow out of his roots: and the spirit of the Lord shall rest upon him, the spirit of wisdom and understanding, the spirit of counsel and might, the spirit of knowledge and of the fear of the Lord; and shall make him of quick understanding in the fear of the Lord: and he shall not judge after the sight of his eyes, neither reprove after the hearing of his ears: but with righteousness shall he judge the poor, and reprove with equity for the meek of the earth: and he shall smite the earth with the rod of his mouth, and with the breath of his lips shall he slay the wicked. And righteousness shall be the girdle of his loins, and faithfulness the girdle of his reins. And in that day there shall be a root of Jesse, which shall stand for an ensign of the people; to it shall the Gentiles seek: and his rest shall be glorious.

And he saw that there was no man, and wondered that there was no intercessor: therefore his arm brought salvation unto him; and his righteousness, it sustained him. For he put on righteousness as a breastplate, and an helmet of salvation upon his head; and he put on the garments of vengeance for clothing, and was clad with zeal as a cloak. And the Redeemer shall come to Zion, and unto them that turn from transgression in Jacob, saith the Lord.

And it shall be said in that day, Lo, this is our God; we have waited for him, and he will save us: this is the Lord; we have waited for him, we will be glad and rejoice in his salvation.

In that day shall this song be sung in the land of Judah; We have a strong city; salvation will God appoint for walls and bulwarks. Open ye the gates, that the righteous nation which keepeth the truth may enter in.

Praise the Lord! Call upon his name! Declare his doings among the people! Make mention that his name is exalted!

Sing unto the Lord; for he hath done excellent things: this is known in all the earth.

Cry out and shout, thou inhabitant of Zion: for great is the Holy One of Israel in the midst of thee.

Taken from: Isa. 40:1-5; 60:1-3; 11:1-5, 10; 59:16-17, 20; 25:9; 26:1-2; 12:4-6

The Christmas Story

This is how the birth of Jesus Christ came about:

God sent the angel Gabriel to Nazareth, a town in Galilee, to a virgin pledged to be married to a man named Joseph, a descendant of David. The virgin's name was Mary. The angel went to her and said,

"Greetings, you who are highly favored! The Lord is with you. You will be with child and give birth to a son, and you are to give him the name Jesus. The Holy Spirit will come upon you, and the power of the Most High will overshadow you. So the holy one to be born will be called the Son of God."

"I am the Lord's servant," Mary answered. "May it be to me as you have said." Then the angel left her.

And Mary [sang]:

"My soul glorifies the Lord and my spirit rejoices in God my Savior, for he has been mindful of the humble state of his servant. From now on all generations will call me blessed, for the Mighty One has done great things for me—holy is his name."

Because Joseph her husband was a righteous man and did not want to expose her to public disgrace, he had in mind to divorce her quietly. But . . . an angel of the Lord appeared to him in a dream and said, "Do not be afraid to take Mary home as your wife, because what is conceived in her is from the Holy Spirit."

When Joseph woke up, he did what the angel of the Lord had commanded him and took Mary home as his wife.

In those days Caesar Augustus issued a decree that a census should be taken of the entire Roman world. And everyone went to his own town to register.

So Joseph also went up from the town of Nazareth in Galilee to Judea, to Bethlehem . . . because he belonged to the house and line of David. He went there to register with Mary, who was pledged to be married to him and was expecting a child. While they were there, the time came for the baby to be born, and she gave birth to her firstborn, a son. She wrapped him in cloths and placed him in a manger, because there was no room for them in the inn.

And there were shepherds living out in the fields nearby, keeping watch over their flocks at night. An angel of the Lord appeared to them, and the glory of the Lord shone around them, and they were terrified. But the angel said to them, "Do not be afraid. I bring you good news of great joy that will be for all the people. Today in the town of David a Savior has been born to you; he is Christ the Lord. This will be a sign to you: You will find a baby wrapped in cloths and lying in a manger."

Suddenly a great company of the heavenly host appeared with the angel, praising God and saying,

"Glory to God in the highest, and on earth peace to men on whom his favor rests."

When the angels had left them and gone into heaven, the shepherds said to one another, "Let's go to Bethlehem and see this thing that has happened, which the Lord has told us about."

So they hurried off and found Mary and Joseph, and the baby, who was lying in the manger. When they had seen him, they spread the word concerning what had been told them about this child, and all who heard it were amazed at what the shepherds said to them.

After Jesus was born in Bethlehem in Judea . . . Magi from the east came to Jerusalem and asked,

"Where is the one who has been born king of the Jews? We saw his star in the east and have come to worship him."

When King Herod heard this he was disturbed, and all Jerusalem with him. When he had called together all the people's chief priests and teachers of the law, he asked them where the Christ was to be born. "In Bethlehem in Judea," they replied, "for this is what the prophet has written."

[Then Herod sent the Magi to Bethlehem to make a careful search for the Child.]

They went on their way, and the star they had seen in the east went ahead of them until it stopped over the place where the child was. When they saw the star, they were overjoyed. On coming to the house, they saw the child with his mother Mary, and they bowed down and worshiped him.

All this took place to fulfill what the Lord had said through the prophet.

Taken from: Matt. 1:18; Luke 1:26-28, 31, 35, 38, 46-49; Matt. 1:19-20, 24; Luke 2:1, 3-18; Matt. 2:1-5, 9-11; 1:22 (all NIV)

The Seven Last Words of Jesus

Lest I forget Gethsemane,
Lest I forget Thine agony,
Lest I forget Thy love for me,
Lead me to Calvary.

When they were come unto a place called Golgotha, they crucified [Jesus], and parted his garments, casting lots. Sitting down they watched him there; and set up over his head his accusation written, THIS IS JESUS THE KING OF THE JEWS.

And they that passed by reviled him, wagging their heads, and saying, Thou that destroyest the temple, and buildest it in three days, save thyself. If thou be the Son of God, come down from the cross.

Likewise also the chief priests mocking him, with the scribes and elders, said, He saved others; himself he cannot save. If he be the King of Israel, let him now come down from the cross, and we will believe him. He trusted in God; let him deliver him now, if he will have him: for he said, I am the Son of God.

Then said Jesus, <u>Father, forgive them; for they know not what they do</u>.

And one of the malefactors which were hanged railed on him, saying, If thou be Christ, save thyself and us. But the other answering rebuked him, saying, Dost not thou fear God, seeing thou art in the same condemnation? And we indeed justly; for we receive the due reward of our deeds: but this man hath done nothing amiss. And he said unto Jesus,

Lord, remember me when thou comest into thy kingdom. And Jesus said unto him, <u>Verily I say unto thee, To day shalt thou be with me in paradise</u>.

When Jesus therefore saw his mother, and the disciple standing by, whom he loved, he saith unto his mother, <u>Woman, behold thy son</u>! Then saith he to the disciple, <u>Behold thy mother</u>! And from that hour that disciple took her unto his own home.

Now from the sixth hour there was darkness over all the land unto the ninth hour. And about the ninth hour Jesus cried with a loud voice, saying, <u>Eli, Eli, lama sabachthani</u>? that is to say, <u>My God, my God, why hast thou forsaken me</u>?

After this, Jesus knowing that all things were now accomplished, that the scripture might be fulfilled, saith, <u>I thirst</u>.

And straightway one of them ran, and took a spunge, and filled it with vinegar, and put it on a reed, and gave him to drink. When Jesus therefore had received the vinegar, he said, <u>It is finished</u>.

And when Jesus had cried with a loud voice, he said, <u>Father, into thy hands I commend my spirit</u>: and having said thus, he gave up the ghost.

Taken from: Matt. 27:33, 35, 36-37, 39-43; Luke 23:34, 39-43; John 19:26-27; Matt. 27:45-46; John 19:28; Matt. 27:48; John 19:30; Luke 23:46

He Is Risen

(While a narrator reads these words, the action could be dramatized in an appropriate setting.)

[It was crucifixion day. The very Son of God had suffered the cruelest form of death—death on a cross.]

As evening approached, there came a rich man from Arimathea, named Joseph, who had himself become a disciple of Jesus. Going to Pilate, he asked for Jesus' body, and Pilate ordered that it be given to him. So Joseph bought some linen cloth, took down the body, wrapped it in the linen, and placed it in his own new tomb that he had cut out of the rock. Then he rolled a stone against the entrance of the tomb. It was Preparation Day, and the Sabbath was about to begin.

The women who had come with Jesus from Galilee followed Joseph and saw the tomb and how his body was laid in it. Then they went home and prepared spices and perfumes. But they rested on the Sabbath in obedience to the commandment.

The next day, the chief priests and the Pharisees went to Pilate. "Sir," they said, "we remember that while he was still alive that deceiver said, 'After three days I will rise again.' So give the order for the tomb to be made secure until the third day. Otherwise, his disciples may come and steal the body and tell the people that he has been raised from the dead. This last deception will be worse than the first."

"Take a guard," Pilate answered. "Go, make the tomb as secure as you know how." So they went and made the tomb secure by putting a seal on the stone and posting the guard.

After the Sabbath, at dawn on the first day of the week
... [t]here was a violent earthquake, for an angel of the Lord
came down from heaven and, going to the tomb, rolled back
the stone and sat on it. His appearance was like lightning,
and his clothes were white as snow. The guards were so
afraid of him that they shook and became like dead men.

Very early in the morning, Mary Magdalene, Mary the
mother of James, and Salome took the spices they had prepared and went to the tomb that they might anoint Jesus'
body. ... On their way to the tomb they asked each other,
"Who will roll the stone away from the entrance of the
tomb?" But when they looked up, they saw that the stone,
which was very large, had been rolled away. But when they
entered, they did not find the body of the Lord Jesus. While
they were wondering about this, suddenly two men in
clothes that gleamed like lightning stood beside them. In
their fright the women bowed down with their faces to the
ground, but the men said to them, "Do not be afraid, ... you
are looking for Jesus, who was crucified. He is not here; he
has risen, just as he said. Remember how he told you, while
he was still with you in Galilee: 'The Son of Man must be
delivered into the hands of sinful men, be crucified and on
the third day be raised again.'" Then they remembered his
words. "Come and see the place where he lay. Then go
quickly and tell his disciples: 'He has risen from the dead and
is going ahead of you into Galilee. There you will see him.'"

So the women hurried away from the tomb, afraid yet
filled with joy, and ran to tell his disciples.

While the women were on their way, some of the guards
went into the city and reported to the chief priests everything
that had happened. When the chief priests had met with the
elders and devised a plan, they gave the soldiers a large sum

of money, telling them, "You are to say, 'His disciples came during the night and stole him away while we were asleep.' If this report gets to the governor, we will satisfy him and keep you out of trouble." So the soldiers took the money and did as they were instructed. And this story [was] widely circulated among the Jews.

When they heard that Jesus was alive, [the disciples] did not believe the women, because their words seemed to them like nonsense.

Peter and the other disciple started for the tomb. Both were running, but the other disciple outran Peter and reached the tomb first. He bent over and looked in at the strips of linen lying there but did not go in. Then Simon Peter, who was behind him, arrived and went into the tomb. He saw the strips of linen lying there, as well as the burial cloth that had been around Jesus' head. The cloth was folded up by itself, separate from the linen. Finally the other disciple, who had reached the tomb first, also went inside. He saw and believed. (They still did not understand from Scripture that Jesus had to rise from the dead.)

Then the disciples went back to their homes, but Mary stood outside the tomb crying. [As] she turned around [she] saw Jesus standing there, but she did not realize that it was Jesus.

"Woman," he said, "why are you crying? Who is it you are looking for?"

Thinking he was the gardener, she said, "Sir, if you have carried him away, tell me where you have put him, and I will get him."

Jesus said to her, "Mary."

She turned toward him and cried out in Aramaic, "Rabboni!" (which means Teacher).

Jesus said, "Do not hold on to me, for I have not yet returned to the Father. Go instead to my brothers and tell them, 'I am returning to my Father and your Father, to my God and your God.'"

Mary Magdalene went to the disciples with the news: "I have seen the Lord!" And she told them that he had said these things to her.

[Afterward Jesus] showed himself to these men . . . over a period of forty days . . . and gave many convincing proofs that he was alive.

> Compiled from the four Gospel accounts: Matthew 27—28; Mark 15—16; Luke 23—24; John 20; and Acts 1:3 (all NIV)

The Suffering Servant and the Triumphant Lord

Behold the Lamb of God, which taketh away the sin of the world.

He [was] despised and rejected of men; a man of sorrows, and acquainted with grief: and we hid as it were our faces from him; he was despised, and we esteemed him not. Surely he hath borne our griefs, and carried our sorrows: yet we did esteem him stricken, smitten of God, and afflicted. But he was wounded for our transgressions, he was bruised for our iniquities: the chastisement of our peace was upon him; and with his stripes we are healed. All we like sheep have gone astray; we have turned every one to his own way; and the Lord hath laid on him the iniquity of us all.

[And he said,] Reproach hath broken my heart; I am full of heaviness: and I looked for some to take pity, but there was none; and for comforters, but I found none.

Yet it pleased the Lord to bruise him; he hath put him to grief: when thou shalt make his soul an offering for sin, he shall see his seed, he shall prolong his days, and the pleasure of the Lord shall prosper in his hand. He shall see of the travail of his soul, and shall be satisfied.

[For he] made himself of no reputation, and took upon him the form of a servant, and was made in the likeness of men: and being found in fashion as a man, he humbled himself, and became obedient unto death, even the death of the cross. Wherefore God also hath highly exalted him, and given him a name which is above every name: that at the name of Jesus every knee should bow . . . and that every tongue should confess that Jesus Christ is Lord, to the glory of God the Father.

I know that my redeemer liveth, and that he shall stand at the latter day upon the earth. [For] now is Christ risen from the dead, and become the firstfruits of them that slept. Since by man came death, by man came also the resurrection of the dead. For as in Adam all die, even so in Christ shall all be made alive.

> Lift up your heads, O ye gates;
> And be ye lift up, ye everlasting doors;
> And the King of glory shall come in.
>
> Who is this King of glory?
>
> The Lord strong and mighty,
> The Lord mighty in battle.
>
> Lift up your heads, O ye gates;
> Even lift them up, ye everlasting doors;
> And the King of glory shall come in.
>
> Who is this King of glory?
>
> The Lord of hosts,
> He the King of glory.

Worthy is the Lamb that was slain, and [hath] redeemed us to God by [his] blood, to receive power, and riches, and wisdom, and strength, and honour, and glory, and blessing.

Blessing, and honour, and glory, and power, be unto him that sitteth upon the throne, and unto the Lamb for ever and ever. Amen.

And I heard a great voice of much people in heaven, saying, Alleluia; Salvation, and glory, and honour, and power, unto the Lord our God.

And I heard as it were the voice of a great multitude, and as the voice of many waters, and as the voice of mighty thunderings, saying, Alleluia: for the Lord God omnipotent reigneth!

> Taken from: John 1:29; Isa. 53:3-6; Ps. 69:20; Isa. 53:10-11; Phil. 2:7-11; Job 19:25; 1 Cor. 15:20-22; Ps. 24:7-10; Rev. 5:12, 9, 13-14; 19:1, 6

The Children of God

As many as received [Jesus], to them gave he power to become the sons of God, even to them that believe on his name: which were born, not of blood, nor of the will of the flesh, nor of the will of man, but of God. Behold, what manner of love the Father hath bestowed upon us, that we should be called the sons of God. Wherefore come out from among them, and be ye separate, saith the Lord ... and I will receive you, and will be a Father unto you, and ye shall be my sons and daughters, saith the Lord Almighty. He that overcometh shall inherit all things; and I will be his God, and he shall be my son.

Ye are of God, little children, and have overcome [that spirit of antichrist]: because greater is he that is in you, than he that is in the world. For ye are all the children of God by faith in Christ Jesus. And if ye be Christ's, then are ye Abraham's seed, and heirs according to the promise.

As many as are led by the Spirit of God, they are the sons of God. For ye have not received the spirit of bondage again to fear; but ye have received the Spirit of adoption, whereby we cry, Abba, Father. The Spirit [himself] beareth witness with our spirit, that we are the children of God: and if children, then heirs; heirs of God, and joint-heirs with Christ. Behold, now are we the sons of God, and it doth not yet appear what we shall be: but we know that, when he shall appear, we shall be like him; [for he said,] I will receive you, and will be a Father unto you, and ye shall be my sons and daughters.

Taken from: John 1:12-13; 1 John 3:1; 2 Cor. 6:17-18; Rev. 21:7; 1 John 4:4; Gal. 3:26, 29; Rom. 8:14-17; 1 John 3:2; 2 Cor. 6:17-18

Freedom in Christ

There is therefore now no condemnation to them which are in Christ Jesus, who walk not after the flesh, but after the Spirit. For the law of the Spirit of life in Christ Jesus hath made me free from the law of sin and death. For they that are after the flesh do mind the things of the flesh; but they that are after the Spirit the things of the Spirit. For to be carnally minded is death; but to be spiritually minded is life and peace. For if ye live after the flesh, ye shall die: but if ye through the Spirit do mortify the deeds of the body, ye shall live. For as many as are led by the Spirit of God, they are the sons of God.

Ye have not received the spirit of bondage again to fear; but ye have received the Spirit of adoption, whereby we cry, Abba, Father. The Spirit [himself] beareth witness with our spirit, that we are the children of God: and if children, then heirs; heirs of God, and joint-heirs with Christ; if so be that we suffer with him, that we may be also glorified together.

Likewise the Spirit also helpeth our infirmities: for we know not what we should pray for as we ought: but the Spirit [himself] maketh intercession for us with groanings which cannot be uttered. And he that searcheth the hearts knoweth what is the mind of the Spirit, because he maketh intercession for the saints according to the will of God. And we know that all things work together for good to them that love God, to them who are the called according to his purpose.

What shall we then say to these things? If God be for us, who can be against us? He that spared not his own Son, but delivered him up for us all, how shall he not with him also freely give us all things?

Who shall separate us from the love of Christ? shall tribulation, or distress, or persecution, or famine, or nakedness, or peril, or sword? Nay, in all these things we are more than conquerors through him that loved us. For I am persuaded, that neither death, nor life, nor angels, nor principalities, nor powers, nor things present, nor things to come, nor height, nor depth, nor any other creature, shall be able to separate us from the love of God, which is in Christ Jesus our Lord.

Romans 8, abridged

Christ's Prayer for Us

In the world ye shall have tribulation: but be of good cheer; I have overcome the world.

These words spake Jesus, and lifted up his eyes to heaven, and said, Father, the hour is come; glorify thy Son, that thy Son also may glorify thee.

I have glorified thee on the earth: I have finished the work which thou gavest me to do.

And now, O Father, glorify thou me with thine own self with the glory which I had with thee before the world was.

I have manifested thy name unto the men which thou gavest me out of the world: thine they were, and thou gavest them me; and they have kept thy word.

I pray for them: I pray not for the world, but for them which thou hast given me; for they are thine.

And all mine are thine, and thine are mine; and I am glorified in them.

And now I am no more in the world, but these are in the world, and I come to thee. Holy Father, keep through thine own name those whom thou hast given me, that they may be one, as we are.

I pray not that thou shouldest take them out of the world, but that thou shouldest keep them from the evil.

They are not of the world, even as I am not of the world.

Sanctify them through thy truth: thy word is truth.

As thou hast sent me into the world, even so have I also sent them into the world.

And for their sakes I sanctify myself, that they also might be sanctified through the truth.

Neither pray I for these alone, but for them also which shall believe on me through their word;

That they all may be one; as thou, Father, art in me, and I in thee, that they also may be one in us: that the world may believe that thou hast sent me.

And the glory which thou gavest me I have given them; that they may be one, even as we are one:

I in them, and thou in me, that they may be made perfect in one; and that the world may know that thou hast sent me, and hast loved them, as thou hast loved me.

John 16:33; 17, abridged

Deliverance in Temptation

Watch and pray, that ye enter not into temptation: the spirit indeed is willing, but the flesh is weak. Wherefore let him that thinketh he standeth take heed lest he fall. We have a great high priest [who] was in all points tempted like as we are, yet without sin.

Jesus was led by the Spirit into the wilderness, being forty days tempted of the devil. And in those days he did eat nothing: and when they were ended, he afterward hungered.

And when the tempter came to him, he said, If thou be the Son of God, command that these stones be made bread. But he answered and said, It is written, Man shall not live by bread alone, but by every word that proceedeth out of the mouth of God.

Then the devil taketh him up into the holy city, and setteth him on a pinnacle of the temple, and saith unto him, If thou be the Son of God, cast thyself down: for it is written, He shall give his angels charge concerning thee: and in their hands they shall bear thee up, lest at any time thou dash thy foot against a stone. Jesus said unto him, It is written again, Thou shalt not tempt the Lord thy God.

Again, the devil taketh him up into an exceeding high mountain, and sheweth him all the kingdoms of the world, and the glory of them; and saith unto him, All these things will I give thee if thou wilt fall down and worship me. Then saith Jesus unto him, Get thee hence, Satan: for it is written, Thou shalt worship the Lord thy God, and him only shalt thou serve. Then the devil leaveth him, and, behold angels came and ministered unto him.

In that [Christ] himself hath suffered being tempted, he is able to [help] them that are tempted. Let no man say when he is tempted, I am tempted of God: for God cannot be tempted with evil, neither tempteth he any man: but every man is tempted, when he is drawn away of his own [desire] and enticed. When the enemy shall come in like a flood, the Spirit of the Lord shall lift up a standard against him. There hath no temptation taken you but such as is common to man: but God is faithful, who will not [allow] you to be tempted above that ye are able; but will with the temptation also make a way to escape, that ye may be able to bear it. The Lord knoweth how to deliver the godly out of temptations.

Put on the whole armour of God, that ye may be able to stand against the wiles of the devil. Resist the devil, and he will flee from you. Draw nigh to God, and he will draw nigh to you. If God be for us, who can be against us? We are more than conquerors through him that loved us.

My brethren, count it all joy when ye fall into divers temptations; knowing this, that the trying of your faith worketh patience. [Wherefore] ye greatly rejoice, though now for a season, if need be, ye are in heaviness through manifold temptations: that the trial of your faith, being much more precious than of gold that perisheth, though it be tried with fire, might be found unto praise and honour and glory at the appearing of Jesus Christ.

Blessed is the man that endureth temptation: for when he is tried, he shall receive the crown of life, which the Lord hath promised to them that love him.

Taken from: Matt. 26:41; 1 Cor. 10:12; Heb. 4:14-15; Luke 4:1-2; Matt. 4:3-11; Heb. 2:18; James 1:13-14; Isa. 59:19; 1 Cor. 10:13; 2 Pet. 2:9; Eph. 6:11; James 4:7-8; Rom. 8:31, 37; James 1:2-3; 1 Pet. 1:6-7; James 1:12

Shadows of Things to Come

Watchman, what of the night? . . . Yet a little while, and he that shall come will come, and will not tarry. . . . It is high time to awake out of sleep: for now is our salvation nearer than when we believed. The night is far spent, the day is at hand: let us therefore cast off the works of darkness, and let us put on the armour of light. . . . Watch and pray always, that ye may be accounted worthy . . . to stand before the Son of man.

Tell us, when shall these things be? and what shall be the sign of thy coming? . . . There shall be signs in the sun, moon, and stars; and upon the earth distress of nations, with perplexity; the sea and the waves roaring; men's hearts failing them for fear, for the powers of heaven shall be shaken.

As the lightning cometh out of the east, and shineth even unto the west; so shall also the coming of the Son of man be.

Learn a parable of the fig tree; When his branch is yet tender, and putteth forth leaves, ye know that summer is nigh: so likewise ye, when ye shall see all these things, know that it is near. . . . The day of the Lord so cometh as a thief in the night. For when they shall say, Peace and safety; then sudden destruction cometh upon them, . . . and they shall not escape. . . . The coming of the Lord draweth nigh. . . . Therefore be ye also ready; for in such an hour as ye think not the Son of man cometh.

[Jesus promised:] In my Father's house are many mansions . . . I go to prepare a place for you. And if I go and prepare a place for you, I will come again, and receive you unto myself; that where I am, there ye may be also.

Be patient therefore, brethren, unto the coming of the Lord. . . . the husbandman waiteth for the precious fruit of the earth, and hath long patience for it, until he receive the early and latter rain. Be ye also patient; stablish your hearts: for the coming of the Lord draweth nigh.

Taken from: Isa. 21:11; Heb. 10:37; Rom. 13:11-12; Luke 21:36; Matt. 24:3; Luke 21:25-26; Matt. 24:27, 32-33; 1 Thess. 5:2-3; James 5:8; Matt. 24:44; John 14:2-3; James 5:7-8

Resurrection to Life Eternal

Christ died for our sins according to the scriptures; and he was buried, and he rose again the third day according to the scriptures.

Now if Christ be preached that he rose from the dead, how say some among you that there is no resurrection of the dead? But if there be no resurrection of the dead, then is Christ not risen: and if Christ be not risen, then is our preaching vain, and your faith is also vain. If in this life only we have hope in Christ, we are of all men most miserable.

But now is Christ risen from the dead, and become the firstfruits of them that slept. For since by man came death, by man came also the resurrection of the dead. For as in Adam all die, even so in Christ shall all be made alive. But some man will say, How are the dead raised up? and with what body do they come? Thou fool, that which thou sowest is not quickened, except it die: and that which thou sowest, thou sowest not that body that shall be, . . . but God giveth it a body as it hath pleased him. So also is the resurrection of the dead. It is sown in corruption; it is raised in incorruption: it is sown in dishonour; it is raised in glory: it is sown in weakness; it is raised in power: it is sown a natural body; it is raised a spiritual body.

Behold, I shew you a mystery; We shall not all sleep, but we shall all be changed, in a moment, in the twinkling of an eye, at the last trump: for the trumpet shall sound, and the dead shall be raised incorruptible, and we shall be changed. For this corruptible must put on incorruption, and this mortal must put on immortality. Then shall be brought to pass the saying that is written, Death is swallowed up in victory.

O death, where is thy sting? O grave, where is thy victory? The sting of death is sin; and the strength of sin is the law. But thanks be to God, which giveth us the victory through our Lord Jesus Christ.

1 Corinthians 15, abridged

www.ingramcontent.com/pod-product-compliance
Lightning Source LLC
Chambersburg PA
CBHW071313110426
42743CB00042B/1472